# The Siamese Cat

Phyllis Lauder

# The Siamese Cat

B. T. BATSFORD LTD London

First published 1971

Printed and bound in Great Britain by
Redwood Burn Limited Trowbridge and Esher
for the publishers B. T. Batsford Ltd.,
4 Fitzhardinge Street, Portman Square, London W1H 0AH
ISBN 0 7134 1733 1

# Contents

Contents

# Illustrations

## Illustrations

# Acknowledgments

In bringing this book up-to-date I have had invaluable help from Mrs Eileen Lentaigne of the Siamese Cat Association; from Mrs Susie Page, well-known writer and judge in the USA; from Madame Pia Hollenstein, President of FIFE; and from Madame la Comtesse Trayer de d'Huizy of France. I am greatly indebted to Mr and Mrs Stephens and the many people in Australia who gave me information; to Mr Cyril Proud, President of the Siamese Cat Society of New Zealand and to J.M. Lifton MRCVS, MACV Sc; and I should like to acknowledge the kindness of Khunying Abhibal Rajamaitri and of the British Embassy in Bangkok.

In Britain I have been helped by the Royal Society for Prevention of Cruelty to Animals, by Mr Turner of Shurlock Row Quarantine Cattery, and by the Ministry of Agriculture.

I should like to record my special gratitude to Sam L. Scheer of the Siamese Cat Society of America for permission to include passages from articles which have appeared in the *Siamese News Quarterly* and for all the help he has given me in collecting information about the Siamese cat fancy in the USA.

I am greatly indebted to the people all over the world who have lent pictures for this book, which I hope is worthy of so much kindness.

Chapter one

# History

No animal was ever higher in man's esteem than the Siamese cat; but it is surprisingly difficult to give a factual account of his early beginnings. It is indeed not easy to discover the origin of any cat. One of the drawbacks to tracing the full story of *felis catus* is that for him there is no prehistory. Fossilised bones of huge saurians or fossil moulds of tiny trilobites enable palaeontologists and archaeologists to reconstruct with certainty a good deal of the history of early life on earth; and the prehistory of man is to be read in the tools that he made and the burials that were carried out by him; many facts of prehistoric times are known to us, and some conjectures are so well founded as to amount to certainty. But for the cat, a small animal leaving his remains above ground, there is no known prehistory.

The earliest cats of which we have record are those of the north-eastern countries of Africa. The ancient Egyptians included certain animals in their theology. The cat, attached to the worship of their goddess Bast or Pasht, was represented in stone or etched into the surface of stone in temples and palaces of old Egypt; he appears with other beasts of the early Egyptian pantheon, his name is written in hieroglyphs, he is buried with pharaohs. This feline of early times closely resembles the cat we know as Abyssinian—with long legs and longish face and, presumably the original wild-type agouti coat-pattern, with banded hairs of yellow, brown and black. (It is incidentally worth noting that the agouti coat-pattern and tabby, lined, blotched or spotted—are not governed by the same gene; thus, tabby and agouti are independent; tabby shows in non-agouti blacks (a ghost pattern), in yellows, whose colour is epistatic over agouti,[1] and also, sometimes, on the flanks of Siamese, who are certainly non-agouti.)

It is commonly believed that northern Africa was the cat's first habitat, from which he travelled all over the world; but this ought not to be regarded as certain and there is no knowing the course of the population migrations involved. There comes a moment in history when we are sure of the existence of a round-faced, sturdy cat in Europe and then, somewhat later, is recorded the presence of a long-faced, slenderly-built cat in the country now known as Thailand. A cat with similar type existed in Abyssinia and Egypt about 3,500 years ago. Although life is known to have come in migratory movements to Europe from the east, the trend being always westward, we are asked to accept that *felis domesticus* originated in Africa, and that among the descendants of the cats of northern Africa was the Siamese. However, 'Morrison-Scott (1951) has shown that the average skull size of mummified Egyptian cats is significantly larger than that of the cats of today'.[2] There is no indication whatever of a time for the arrival of cats in any of the places they now inhabit; they did not cross the land passage which is now the Behring Strait, and which led to the Americas; neither the American Indians nor the Maoris in Australasia knew the domestic cat until the white man came to their shores. Cats appear in recorded history first in Africa, then in Europe and in the east, and they were probably in existence during the mesozoic era, but there is no proof of it. The round-headed, deep-chested cat of western Europe is so different from the slender, long-legged Siamese that it is tempting to think of the one sheltering behind man's cave fires in the west while the other killed rats for his living in the east, both being quite unrelated. But in fact, the early evolution of the cat is not known.

Towards the close of the nineteenth century Europeans discovered Siamese cats in Bangkok and at other places in what was then called Siam. They were quite clearly felines of the same species as the European cats, and Mr Owen Gould brought a pair to England in 1884. This is the first known authentic record. In this year there existed no register, but the cats were written about and discussed in catalogues and journals by the small band of fanciers who saw them when Mr Gould exhibited them. Their arrival was placed on record by the late Cyril Yeates, for many years chairman of the Governing Council of the Cat Fancy, who tells us, among other things, that they were first exhibited at the Crystal Palace in 1895. Their appearance was striking and they were sufficiently different from the western cats to excite a good deal of comment. The unusual coat-pattern produced by the restriction of colour to the points, the vivid blue eyes, the deep voice and the great liking of these cats for human companionship caused a sensation. This was the start of a success story which has been recorded step by step, but it did not lead to knowledge of the origins of this cat. There is a tremendous quantity of legends about Siamese; these are of the fairy-tale order, many of them charming; and nearly all of them attribute to the cats a magical quality. In fact, there must at some stage in the development of the breed have occurred a mutation which produced the spectacular coat-pattern; genetically, the Siamese belongs to the albino series (C). He is a seal-brown animal whose colour, by reason of a factor connected with the gene which governs the temperature mechanism, can show in the phenotype only at the cooler extremities. But he is not an albino; true albinism involves total loss of pigment granules: an albino cat would have white fur and pink eyes, and no colour anywhere; an individual whose eyes are yellow, brown or blue is not a true albino.

There is very little doubt that these cats were at one time admired in Siam; but there has been exaggeration in speaking of them as always being housed in temples and palaces. In fact, there are in Bangkok dozens of princes all of whom style their residences palaces;[3] indeed, not only princes but high officials so describe their houses. In view of this it might be a mistake to suppose that 'imported from the royal palace, Bangkok', written on an early pedigree form, indicates that the cat concerned came from the imperial residence.

However, Sir Owen O'Malley, whose father was Chief Justice in the Malay Settlement from 1889 to 1892, remembers that when he was a very small boy his mother received as a present from the emperor of Siam two Siamese cats, Jemma, male, and Mitsubishie, female, both seal-pointed: 'It must, I think, . . . be about 1890 that the cats named above were brought to Dentons House, Oxfordshire.'[4] This is another authenticated record. It is worth noting that Sir Owen does not state that the cats were resident in the emperor's palace, but only that they were a present from him to Lady O'Malley with whom, since she was the wife of a man of importance, he was bound to be acquainted. It may indeed be that it was left to the West to discover the unusual attributes of these cats; the common-or-garden cat in Siam is said to be, as in the West, the tabby. It is also said that the commonly seen cats today in Bangkok are those whom we call Burmese; Siamese are now rare, and are sometimes supposed to have been brought into the country by Europeans! 'The exact origin of the Siamese cat is apparently a debated point in Bangkok.'[5] Very early importers of cats from Siam spoke and wrote of them as being of two varieties: the Royal, which was what we call a seal-pointed Siamese, and the Chocolate, which was a brown-all-over animal with points darker than the coat and with, very often, golden eyes. From this it seems clear that the cats considered at the end of the nineteenth century to be Siamese of two kinds were in fact the blue-eyed cats with the restriction-of-colour-to-points factor which we designate Siamese, and the yellow-eyed, dark cats which we call Burmese. On the other hand, 'Korats . . . are what the Thai thinks of when you mention Siamese cats.'[6] There is thus considerable confusion about the origins of the cats. It is natural for someone who finds an unusual animal in a particular country to associate the animal with the country and to conclude that this is its place of origin; but Thailand is not an island, it is part of a considerable land mass; our Siamese and Burmese cats have no doubt been able to move across this or that frontier for a long time, and it would be impossible to prove that either is certainly indigenous to this or that country. However, with the records of the arrival of these cats in the West, first in 1884, then in 1890, begin the known and authenticated facts.

Siamese cats first appeared in the United States of America at approximately the same time as they did in England. American ailurophiles, visiting friends in Britain, were taken with the new arrivals and brought some home, afterwards importing more, both from England and from Siam, where tourists, sailors, diplomats and people with business interests were able to collect the cats and bring them home, just as had the British.

The world to which the cats came was entirely different from that of today. Their owners were pleasant, gentle people for whom their cats were a hobby, and who were not in need of money nor interested in self-advancement in the cat world. When they arranged a cat show they hoped, naturally, that their own pet would win a prize, but 'pet' was the operative word: the cats were the cherished pets of their owners. They were often apple-headed, and they were in no danger of being run over; but they could contract ailments from some of which, such as the dreaded feline infectious enteritis (discussed in Chapter 5), they died. Their owners were heartbroken, but they did not know how to deal with the situation.

In trying to trace past events it is essential to have access to reputable recorded dates and facts. These, in respect of the very first

Siamese in America, are simply not available. There was, in the last two decades of the nineteenth century, no registration: who would think of such a thing among the folk who owned these charming pets? The formation of a register was for the future. Petty arguments take place nowadays as to the name of the first person to own such a cat in the USA, or the question whether the first Siamese to come to the West was taken to England or to America. It is the opinion of informed Americans that these questions can never be answered; however, valuable work on the subject of Siamese cat history in America has been done by Charles A. Kenny. His findings appeared in *Cats Magazine* of February—July, 1949; and the *Siamese News Quarterly,* the organ of the Siamese Cat Society of America (see chapter 9), has, with the permission of the publisher of *Cats Magazine*, Raymond D. Smith of Washington, Pennsylvania, reprinted his findings.

Charles A. Kenny, relying on old journals and periodicals, found a lot of blind alleys. 'There have been many writers who have given the name of the individual whom they believe to be the first Siamese cat owner; however, their statements have proven to be incorrect. To prove this point, an article appeared in the July 1909 issue of *The Cat Review,* titled "The Siamese cat", and written by Harold Bassett. In this feature, Mr Bassett is quite emphatic in his statement that Mme Blanche Arral of Grantwood, N.J. was the first person to bring a Siamese cat to America. Mme Arral herself, writing in a 1911 issue of the *Cat Journal* states that the first Siamese she ever saw was in Siam while on a concert tour there in 1902. Volume 1 of the Beresford Cat Club stud book and register published in 1900 contains the listings of two American owned Siamese cats.'[7]

In this way, early history may be bedevilled by statements which cannot be substantiated. However, the research undertaken by *Cats Magazine* gives us our first bit of firm ground. Volume 1 of the Beresford records, issued in July, 1900, registers the names of two Siamese cats, Lockhaven Siam, male, and Lockhaven Sally Ward, female, dates of birth and ancestry listed as unknown, owner Mrs Clinton Locke of Chicago. Thus we know that there were Siamese cats in America before 1900. From the point of view of the breeder, the names and descriptions of cats are of far greater importance than the names of their owners, although these are also of interest. The Beresford records, which amount to registration, are of great importance; the second volume lists two chocolate Siamese, Netherland Tilu and Netherland Ma, born in 1897 and purchased by Mrs Locke from Lady Marcus Beresford. Volume 3 lists a cat born in America, whose sire was Lockhaven Siam and the date of birth of whose dam is given as 1894. This volume also has the name of Madison Calif, an early Siamese champion in America. In those days, the cats had to compete with domestic shorthairs, yet they earned a great many awards: a Siamese, Lockhaven Elsa, was best cat in an all-breed show judged by Louis Wain in 1908.

Our authority gives the names of well-known breeders who fostered the then new breed; they include Mrs Locke, Mme Arral and Miss Cathcart as well as Mrs Dykehouse, and such well-known names as those of Dr G. D. Hindley, Mrs Mathis and, a little later on, Mrs Virginia Cobb. These people, who fought hard to establish the lovely breed, had to contend with the enteritis which took such a toll of their stock, and also with in-breeding. Litters were small and breeders consulted with their English friends whose cats did not suffer so greatly in this respect; it is to be supposed that more Siamese were at first imported into England, some of them unrelated. People paid a thousand dollars for a Siamese from England, and this with the very big risk of losing it. It was a leisured, monied class which established, at great cost in money and effort, these delightful cats; but it was not until veterinary science took a hand that these dedicated breeders could feel any degree of safety.

One of the imports was Mrs Dykehouse's female, bought from Mrs Chilcott, and a daughter of champion Kew King of Siam, whose name appears on many an old pedigree. The importance of records becomes clear when the matter of a cat's descent arises. The data collected by *Cats Magazine* include, for example, the information that on 10-12 August 1925 at Vancouver, best-in-the-show was a Siamese male called Mon Dek Lik; in the pedigree of a truly beautiful cat born in 1933 in England appears among his grandparents the name of Champion Mon Dek. There are two pictures of the early cats available: Champion Lady Sonia, listed in the CFA stud book's third volume, who was best cat in the Atlantic City Club's show in New York City in January, 1913; and champion Siam de Paris, America's first Siamese champion, who was at least once best cat in show. To judge by their photographs, Lady Sonia is a comfortable podge with a shocking squint, and Siam de Paris has a head that looks as if it would do credit to a domestic shorthair, besides being as fat as butter! But both pictures show really dense points, and a marked colour-contrast. We have to remember, besides, that those were the days when 'puss' was judged by weight! These two competed against all the cats in the shows—longhairs as well as shorthairs. 'To date we have found in our research that in the 54-year history of the American cat fancy only 15 Siamese have won the title of best cat in an all-breed sanctioned exhibition.'[8] Sanctioned, in America, has not the same meaning as in Britain, where a 'sanction show' (see Chapter 6) is not a championship show, but has nevertheless the blessing of the Governing Council; in America, a sanctioned show is a full championship show, approved by the governing body concerned.

In tracing the story of the Siamese fancy, *Cats Magazine* collaborators found the usual difficulty—there were few written records. Thanks to *The Cat Review*, however, it is clearly established that the Siamese Cat Society of America was founded in 1909; the big names of the early years appear in this record: Mrs Dykehouse, President, Mrs G. E. Taylor, Secretary and Treasurer, Mrs Clinton Locke, Honorary President. The new Society, modelled at first on the Siamese Cat Club with which it had close associations, and then formulating its own standards, did not immediately prosper, for the circumstances of the times were against it. Later, such names as those of Mrs Naatz and Mrs Cobb came into prominence; this Society remained, despite some disagreements as to standards, on good terms with the Cat Fanciers Association, together with which it staged the first Siamese specialty show in America at Detroit in 1928.

In South Africa , the first cat show took place in 1949. The Siamese cat, so popular now in the Union, was comparatively lately imported.

The Siamese fancy was not established in New Zealand until the early 1950's. Before that, the cats had a history of ill-health almost certainly caused by inbreeding; they were very rare, and a clowder was kept at the Auckland Zoo, where kittens, and a stud service, could be arranged for. Then imports from England were obtained by well-known New Zealand fanciers such as Mrs Downey in Auckland who, with others, imported some of the famous Doneraile cats; and Mr Moran of Wellington to whom went Killdown Jupiter, one of the most beautiful, strong, seal-pointed males I ever saw. These cats brought new vigour to the N.Z. Siamese, and saved them to become the lovely creatures they are now. Since that time, imports of all points-colours have arrived, and very careful breeding programmes have been carried out. 'From the six Siamese cats at the first Auckland all-breed show held in 1950, the first one after the war, Siamese cats are represented in their hundreds at the many cat shows held throughout New Zealand.'[9] It is wonderful what has been achieved in a comparatively short time.

The cats had come to Australia only a short while earlier. The Siamese Cat Club of Australia held, in 1950, 'A first show and a more imposing array of cups and trophies you never did see! They would have done credit to a veteran club. The show opened at noon and so quickly did visitors arrive that . . . it became necessary to instal a member permanently at the microphone to beg, beseech and almost order the crowd . . . to keep moving. For the majority this was the first sight of a Siamese cat. . . . The newest arrivals were sleek and lovely, with such elegant tails and pale body-colour.'[10].

One Australian show was held in Paddington Town Hall; it is amusing to remember that Paddington Baths, in London, was the venue for some of the shows of the 1940s!

One point on which there has been doubt is the matter of the introduction of blue into the points of these cats—in fact, the origin of the blue-points. The cats that came to the West during the final years of the last century and the first years of the present century were all of them seal-points, and it was found that some, though by no means all of these could produce blue-pointed kittens. Blue is one of the dilutions of eumelanin, and it is supposed that the gene for blue dilution was introduced into the Siamese by a natural cross with a blue-all-over jungle cat of Malaysia. This is the theory: the self-blue cats exist in Malaysia; they could at any reasonably recent era have crossed the Isthmus of Kra into Korat, where there is a very charming self-blue cat with lime-green eyes like peridots and some silvering of the coat, which has recently been established as a separate breed, known as the Korat cat, in America. Once in Korat, the self-blues could naturally have advanced into Siam, where could have occurred the crosses which produced the blue-pointed Siamese. This is conjecture. Nowadays, the breeding of fancy cats is controlled: we have taken it upon ourselves to arrange their matings, and these are recorded by the registration of kittens. But in ancient days there were of course no records but those of fossils and burial places. No one saw a self-blue cat come into Siam from the south, no one witnessed his mating with a seal-pointed Siamese. But although it cannot be proved that this was the manner in which the blue-points came into being, the blue Malay cat is there and the dilution came from somewhere; so this is a reasonable assumption, and probably at least not far from the truth.

When these cats were brought to Europe and to America fanciers were not slow to form associations for them: the Siamese Cat Club, the largest specialist cat club in the world, was founded in 1901, and the Siamese Cat Society of America in 1908. The first Siamese to arrive in the West had points which were sometimes seal-brown and sometimes seal-black; even today, you may occasionally see a cat or kitten with truly black points. Perhaps these are the cats who do not carry the gene for brown dilution of eumelanin. This is, again, a dilution whose origin is not known; indeed the conjecture, often made, that it came from a brown-all-over animal is less convincing than the theory put forward to explain the blue-pointeds: this latter has the advantage of being an informed guess, whereas the self-brown ancestor of the chocolate-points is conspicuous by his absence —unless the Burmese, with his many differences of conformation and colour, is to be considered. The early breeders knew the chocolate-points before the appearance of the blue-points. The significant point is that when the seal-pointeds arrived in Europe and in America, some of them carried the factor for blue dilution, and a good many carried that for chocolate: thus they already, although the fact was not then appreciated, had the necessary genotype for the evolution of lilac-points: those beautiful Siamese which were only, in the first instance, able to be bred from two cats who both had chocolate and both had blue in their ancestry.

The introduction, much later in their history, of tabby and red into their points was nearly always from controlled matings organised by man, and whereas both chocolate and blue are dilutions of eumelanin (black), tabby and red were new to the breed: indeed, red comes from phaeomelanin. However, the two early dilutions were certainly 'sparked off' by crosses with blue and brown cats; just as were the red-points and tabby-points by crosses with red cats and tabby cats.

The arrival of Siamese in England and America marked the beginning of reliable history of the breed because the people who owned them wished to register their kittens. Siamese went to America either direct from Thailand or via Britain at the end of the nineteenth century; it was a time when people were beginning to be 'ailurophile', and the fanciers in both Britain and America were quick in deciding to keep registers of the kittens they bred, thus recording pedigrees. The cats travelled in leisurely fashion to Europe, to Canada, South Africa, New Zealand and Australia. They did not become popular overnight: 'The first annual show of the newly-formed Siamese Cat Club of Australia held 24 June 1950 was a wonderful success. The chinchillas, the blues, the smokes etc. were all wonderful I do not doubt. Being a Siamese fan I seem unable to appreciate all their qualities, but I did see a newly-imported Russian blue, the first of its kind in Australia, which had great attraction and distinct personality. These could run the Siamese closely, I should think.'[11]

Thus, nearly 30 years ago, the secretary of Australia's Siamese Cat Club clearly did not realise what a cult the fancy for Siamese was to become. By the end of the decade, Siamese cats were embroidered on handkerchiefs, and appeared on Christmas cards, calendars, picture postcards and finally tea-towels; there were Siamese in a Walt Disney picture, Siamese on nursery crockery; people all over the world wished to own them; a pet Siamese was said to have become a status symbol. Such is their popularity with breeders that we often see the introduction of Siamese into other varieties: the beautiful colourpoints with their 'persian' type and their lovely long coats are neither more nor less than longhair Siamese; breeders have worked and waited to blend the various characteristics—the long fur, the Siamese pattern, the sturdy type—into a lovely cat; first appearing as a come-by-chance Siamese with long fur, the colourpoint is now a fine longhair—with the admired and coveted coat-pattern. (See p. 44).

The cats called Birmans are also longhair Siamese—longhair cats carrying Siamese plus the factor for white spotting, which gives them their white feet. These have brilliant blue eyes—something that has been lost in the colourpoints. When the latter were first established, the best longhairs available were used, mostly blues and blacks with deep eye-colour. The result was the well-known 'Himmie'—the Himalayan of the USA, which is the colourpoint of the rest of the world, established by the late B. A. Stirling-Webb and some of his American friends from 'Georgie', the longhair Siamese whose home was, briefly, with me. He told me that he intended to produce a cat with good longhair type, and he succeeded—but the brilliant blue of the Siamese eyes was lost, and the eyes of the colourpoints are almost always pale. The reason is that the deep orange of the good longhairs is present in the iris, and precludes the blue from penetrating fully from the lower layer to the iris. Where the Birmans are concerned, longhair type was not desired, but only the length of coat: the face of a good Birman is pointed; any longhairs used in their breeding did not have to be gloriously-typed cats with strong eye-colour, and thus the deep blue is able to show. Mary Batten, the distinguished geneticist from Queensland, remarks that the best ancestor for a colourpoint would have been a longhair with magnificent type and very poor eye-colour! An unlikely combination![12]

Besides the longhairs, there are the shorthairs derived from Siamese: the whites, with coats like ermine and lovely blue eyes; the Havanas (self-chocolates), the lilacs, ebonies and blues, all with lime-green eyes; these have been given various names, as 'foreign shorthairs', 'exotics', 'self-Siamese', 'oriental shorthairs' and, in the case of the tabby with Siamese type, 'Egyptian Mau'. They can appear in any of the colours found in the points of Siamese, and they are simply cats of Siamese type with the colour *not* restricted to the points.

The rex-coated cats, with their delightful, wavy, soft fur, had not been long on the scene before they were crossed with Siamese, and there were seen in the show pens si-rex, with pale, waved coats and vivid blue eyes. Here the work involved for the breeders was made easier by the fact that rex, especially Cornish rex, have naturally got 'foreign' type, so that there were comparatively quickly produced some charming cats with blue eyes, coloured points, slinky, long-legged type and wavy fur—rex with the desired Siamese coat-pattern. To know if any particular variety will blend with Siamese has become a matter of importance: this is the measure of their popularity.

Plenty of people who have no interest in the heredity or the history of the cats yet fall victims to their mystique, and Siamese are both bred and owned as pets all over the world. Their appearance is so unusual, their devotion to their owners so great that this is not to be wondered at. The breed has supplanted all others in popular favour. Siamophiles write to each other from the north of Finland to the south of New Zealand; the efforts of international bodies to achieve unity among nations could succeed in half-a-day if the persons concerned all knew and loved Siamese cats! This is not a joke. Eastern people can write reams to a westerner about the various aspects of breeding Siamese, and when the westerner replies, he never stops to wonder how many guns are stacked in his correspondent's country—he simply is not interested. Someone corresponding with another Siamese cat lover from afar might well think that if their countries should go to war with each other, then that pleasant young man who loves his Siamese so much would have to become a soldier and an enemy—and what would become of his cats? Siamese cats, have, in far less than a century, circled the world; they are very good ambassadors and real interest in them knows, like science, no frontiers.

Chapter two

# Standards, changes and variations: I

Siamese cats have altered considerably since they came to the west in the closing years of the nineteenth century. They would have changed, slowly, as time passed, even if they had not left their native heath nor been fostered by any human being, for evolution is a series of small, discontinuous variations; but when man took a hand in their breeding and rearing the process of change was accelerated. In caring for the cats we have altered their surroundings, which are no longer the ones they knew in the wild, nor in the cities of Siam; and in organising breeding programmes for them, we have become selective agents for their progeny—though it would be a mistake to suppose that our interference with the affairs of the Siamese cat has anything artificial about it. We give the name artefact to an object made by human hands, and we tend much too easily to forget that man is part of nature; his highly diversified brain has developed just as have the horse's power of speed and the bird's wings; and his interest in animals with all the arrangements that he makes for them are part of the same process of evolution: when man makes a block of flats he is no more unnatural than is the beaver when he builds a lodge; he is simply fulfilling his destiny.

However, our intervention in the lives of Siamese cats has undoubtedly produced effects not precisely the same as those which would have come about without us, and it has also hastened the process of change. In fact there have occurred, well within a century, definite alterations and a surprising number of new varieties. Standards of points are drawn up by committees; they are discussed at length and when they are issued, they embody the characteristics most admired by the committee concerned, and they are the basis for the judging of the cats at shows, and the blueprint for breeders.

BRITISH STANDARDS

Here are the British standards for the breeds numbered 24, 24a, 24b and 24c:

*Siamese (Seal-pointed) Breed* 24

*Shape (body and tail).* Medium in size, body long and svelte, legs proportionately slim, hind legs slightly higher than the front ones, feet small and oval, tail long and tapering and free from any kink. A visible kink shall disqualify.
*Head and ears.* Head long and well proportioned, with width between the eyes, narrowing in perfectly straight lines to a fine muzzle. Ears rather large and pricked, wide at the base.
*Eyes (colour and shape).* Clear, brilliant deep blue, shape Oriental and slanting towards the nose. No tendency to squint.
*Body colour.* Cream, shading gradually into pale warm fawn on the back. Kittens paler in colour.
*Points.* Mask, ears, legs, feet and tail dense and clearly defined seal brown. Mask complete (except in kittens) connected by tracing with the ears.
*Coat.* Very short and fine in texture, glossy and close-lying.

NOTES AND DEFINITIONS

*Definition of squint*: When the eyes are so placed that they appear to look permanently at the nose.

VALUE OF POINTS

| *Type and Shape* | | *Colour* | |
|---|---|---|---|
| Head | 15 | Eyes | 15 |
| Ears | 5 | Points | 10 |
| Eyes | 5 | Body colour | 10 |
| Body | 15 | Texture of Coat | 10 |
| Legs and paws | 5 | Condition | 5 |
| Tail | 5 | | |
| TOTAL | 50 | TOTAL | 50 |

*Notes.* The Siamese cat should be a beautifully balanced animal with head, ears and neck carried on a long svelte body, supported on fine legs and feet with a tail in proportion. The head and profile should be wedge shaped, neither round nor pointed. The mask complete, connected by tracings with the ears (except in kittens), the eyes a deep blue, green tinge to be considered a fault. Expression alert and intelligent. White toes or toe automatically to disqualify an exhibit. It is important to note that the standard with regard to Type and Shape is the same for all Siamese cats.

### *Siamese (Blue-pointed) Breed 24a*

The standard is the same as for the seal-pointed with the following exceptions:
*Colour*: Points blue; the ears, mask, legs, paws and tail to be the same colour. The ears should not be darker than the other points.
*Eyes*: Clear, bright, vivid blue.
*Body*: Body colour: glacial white, shading gradually into blue on back, the same cold tone as the points but of a lighter shade.
*Texture of coat*: The same as for seal-pointed.

### *Siamese (Chocolate-pointed) Breed 24b*

The standard is the same as for seal-pointed with the following exceptions:
*Colour*: Points milk chocolate; the ears, mask, paws, legs and tail to be the same colour, the ears should not be darker than the other points.
*Eyes*: Clear, bright, vivid blue
*Body*: Ivory colour all over. Shading, if at all, to be the colour of points.
*Texture of coat*: The same as for seal-pointed.

### *Siamese (Lilac-pointed) Breed 24c*

The standard is the same as for seal-pointed with the following exceptions:
*Eyes*: Clear, light vivid blue.
*Points*: Pinkish grey nose leather and pads faded lilac.
*Body colour*: Magnolia; shading, if any, to tone with points.

*Texture of coat*: As for all Siamese.
Number of points to be awarded for any feature to be the same as for all Siamese.

AMERICAN STANDARDS

The corresponding standards from CFA and ACA (1977) are as follows:

*Cat Fanciers Association*
*Siamese Standards*

POINT SCORE

| | | |
|---|---|---|
| *Head* | | |
| Long flat profile | 6 | |
| Wedge, fine muzzle, size | 5 | |
| Ears | 4 | |
| Chin | 3 | |
| Width between eyes | 2 | 20 |
| *Eyes* | | |
| Shape, size, slant and placement | 10 | 10 |
| *Body* | | |
| Structure and size, including neck | 12 | |
| Muscle tone | 10 | |
| Legs and feet | 5 | |
| Tail | 3 | 30 |
| *Coat* | 10 | 10 |
| *Colour* | | |
| Body colour | 10 | |
| Point colour—matching Points of dense colour, proper foot pads and nose leather | 10 | |
| Eye colour | 10 | 30 |
| | | 100 |

*General*: The ideal Siamese is a svelte, dainty cat with long, tapering lines, very lithe but muscular.
*Head*: Long tapering wedge. Medium size in good proportion to body. The total wedge starts at the nose and flares out in straight

lines to the tips of the ears forming a triangle, with no break at the whiskers. No less than the width of an eye between the eyes. When the whiskers are smoothed back, the underlying bone structure is apparent. Allowance must be made for jowls in the stud cat.
*Skull*: Flat. In profile, a long straight line is seen from the top of the head to the tip of the nose. No bulge over eyes. No dip in nose.
*Nose*: Long and straight. A continuation of the forehead with no break.
*Muzzle*: Fine, wedge-shaped.
*Chin and jaw*: Medium size. Tip of chin lines up with tip of nose in the same vertical plane. Neither receding nor excessively massive.
*Ears*: Strikingly large, pointed, wide at base, continuing the lines of the wedge.
*Eyes*: Almond shaped. Medium size. Neither protruding nor recessed. Slanted towards the nose in harmony with lines of wedge and ears. Uncrossed.
*Body*: Medium size. Dainty, long, and svelte. A distinctive combination of fine bones and firm muscles. Shoulders and hips continue same sleek lines of body. Hips never wider than shoulders. No flaring ribs. Abdomen tight.
*Neck*: Long and slender.
*Legs*: Long and slim. Hind legs higher than front. In good proportion to body.
*Paws*: Dainty, small, and oval. Toes, five in front and four behind.
*Tail*: Long, thin tapering to a fine point.
*Coat*: Short, fine textured, glossy. Lying close to body.
*Condition*: Excellent physical condition. Eyes clear. Muscular strong and lithe. Neither flabby nor boney. Not fat.
*Penalize*: Improper (i.e. off-colour or spotted) nose leather or paw-pads.
*Disqualify*: Any evidence of illness or poor health. Weak hind legs. Mouth breathing due to nasal obstruction or poor occlusion. Emaciation. Visible kink. Eyes other than blue. White toes and/or feet. Incorrect number of toes.
*Colour. Body*: Even, with subtle shading when allowed. Allowance should be made for darker colour in older cats as Siamese generally darken with age, but there must be a definite contrast between body colour and points.
*Points*: Mask, ears, legs, feet, tail dense and clearly defined. All of the same shade. Mask covers entire face including whisker pads and

is connected to ears by tracings. Mask should not extend over top of head. No ticking or white hairs on points.

*Siamese Colours*

*Seal-point*: Body even pale fawn to cream, warm in tone, shading gradually into lighter colour on the stomach and chest. Points deep seal brown.

*Nose leather*: Same colours as points.
*Paw pads*: Same colour as points.
*Eyes*: Deep vivid blue.

*Chocolate-point*: body ivory with no shading. Points milk chocolate colour, warm in tone.

*Nose leather*: Cinnamon pink.
*Paw pads*: Cinnamon pink.
*Eye colour*: Deep vivid blue.

*Blue-point*: Body bluish white, cold in tone, shading gradually to white on stomach and chest. Points deep blue.

*Nose leather*: Slate coloured.
*Paw pads*: Slate coloured.
*Eye colour*: Deep vivid blue.

*Lilac-point*: Body glacial white with no shading. Points frosty grey with pinkish tone.

*Nose leather*: Lavender-pink.
*Paw pads*: Lavender-pink.
*Eye colour*: Deep vivid blue.

*The American Cat Association*
*Siamese Standards 1977*

POINT ALLOTMENT

| | |
|---|---|
| Head | 20 |
| Eyes (colour—5, placement—5) | 10 |
| Ears | 5 |
| Neck and body | 20 |
| Legs and feet | 5 |
| Tail | 5 |
| Coat | 10 |
| Colour (body—5, points—10) | 15 |
| Condition | 10 |
| | 100 |

1 Tabby-point kitten "Hiltonian Caraway" and red-point cat "Moonfleet Caprice", both belonging to Mr and Mrs M P McGinity, London, England

2 Red-points "Rosita van de Felixhoeva" and "Flippa von Nang-sita". Owner: Mme. H Mayr, Blouay, Switzerland

3 Seal-point owned by Mrs R K Atwell of Tulsa, Oklahoma, USA

4 Grand Champion lilac-point "Ophir's Leo", owned and bred by Harry and Mary Lou Nolan of Atlanta, Georgia, USA

5 Chocolate-point "Erol von Ratua-Devi", belonging to Mme. H Mayr of Blouay, Switzerland

6 Chocolate and blue-pointed Siamese, belonging to C A Adriaanse of Amsterdam, Holland

*General Description* : The ideal Siamese is a svelte, dainty cat with long tapering lines, very lithe but muscular.

*Head*

*Shape* : Long tapering wedge.
*Size* : Medium size in good proportion to body.
*Muzzle* : Fine wedge-shaped. The total wedge starts at the nose and flares in straight lines to the tips of the ears forming a triangle, with no break at the whiskers. No less than the width of an eye between the eyes. Whiskers should be smoothed back to determine underlying bone structure. Allowance must be made for jowls, in a stud cat.
*Nose* : Long and straight, a continuation of the forehead with no break.
*Skull* : Flat. In profile, a long straight line is seen from the top of the head to the tip of the nose. No bulge over the eyes. No dip in the nose.
*Chin and jaw* : Medium size. Tip of chin lines up with tip of nose in the same vertical plane. Neither receding or excessively massive.
*Ears* : Strikingly large, pointed, wide at base, continuing the lines of the wedge.

*Body*

*Size* : Medium size. Males slightly larger tnan proper-sized females.
*Body structure* : Dainty long and svelte. A distinctive combination of fine bones and firm muscles. Shoulders and hips continue same sleek lines of body. Hips never wider than shoulders. No flaring of lower ribs. Abdomen tight.
*Legs* : Long and slim. Hind legs higher than front. In good proportion to body.
*Feet* : Dainty, small oval shaped.
*Neck* : Long and slender.
*Tail* : Long, and thin at base, tapering to a fine point, and free from vertebral defect.
*Coat* : Short, fine-textured, glossy, lying close to body.

*Eyes*

Deep, vivid blue. Almond shaped. Medium size. Not protruding. Slanted toward the nose in harmony with lines of wedge and ears. Placed well within the frontal plane of the face. Uncrossed.

*Colour*

*Body colour*: Must harmonize with point colour. Allowance should be made for darker colours on older cats, but there must be definite contrast between body colour and points.
*Point colour*: Mask, ears, legs, feet and tail, dense and clearly defined. All of same shade. Mask covers the centre of the face including whisker pads and is connected to ears by tracing. Mask should not extend over top of head. No ticking or white hairs in points.
*Colour classes*: Determined by point colour. The body colour, point colour, foot pads and nose leather must all harmonize. Each colour must be distinct and definite. No cat may appear to be a blend of two or more colour classes. All colours compete on an equal basis with no allowance for any one colour being more difficult to achieve than another.

*Condition*

Firmly muscled, good coat, bright clear eyes, alert, coat smooth and close-lying.

*Withhold winners*: Wrong foot pad and nose leather colour, eyes any colour other than blue.
*Disqualify*: Any evidence of illness or poor health, any physical abnormality such as weak hind legs, mouth breathing due to nasal obstruction or poor occlusion, etc., emaciation, visible kink, crossed eyes.

*Colour classes*

*Lilac-point*: Body glacial white with no shading. Points frosty grey with pinkish tone, decidedly paler than blue. Foot pads and nose leather lavender-pink. Eyes blue.
*Blue-point*: Body bluish white, cold in tone, shading gradually to

pure white on stomach and chest. Points deep blue-grey. Foot pads and nose leather slate coloured. Eyes blue.

*Chocolate-point*: Body ivory with no shading. Points milk-chocolate colour, warm in tone, decidedly lighter than seal. Foot pads and nose leather cinnamon pink. Eyes blue.

*Seal-point*: Body even pale fawn to cream, warm in tone, shading gradually into lighter colour on stomach and chest. Points deep seal brown to black. Foot pads and nose leather same colour as points. Eyes blue.

*Red-point*: Body colour creamy white. Shading to lighter colour on stomach and chest. Points should be apricot red. Foot pads and nose leather rose pink.

*Tortie-point*: Body colour should be as even as possible, shading gradually into lighter tones on the stomach and chest, conforming to point colours, but always in warm tones. Points should be clearly defined in any one, two, or three colours, with combinations preferred. A 'blaze' may appear on the mask. Nose leather and foot pads to be in any one, two, or three point colours, with combinations preferred. Point colours: lilac with red and/or cream; blue with red and/or cream; chocolate with red and/or cream; seal with red and/or cream. Eyes: blue.

*Lynx-point*: Body colour shades into lighter tones on stomach and chest with no stripes or mottling. Colour conforms to point colour. Points: tabby pattern with interbands clearly defined on mask, legs, feet and tail. Ears clearly outlined with thumb print (lighter area) on back, and tufts on tips. Feet webbed with tracings between the toes. Tail evenly ringed with a dark tip. Nose leather brick red outlined with point colour, or solid in the colour of the points. Paw pads conform to point colour. Point colours: lilac lynx point; blue lynx point; chocolate lynx point; seal lynx point. Eyes: blue.

It will be seen that these do not differ in essence from the European standard, although CFA no longer allots any marks for condition; there is in fact no great difference of opinion as to what constitutes a good standard of points for Siamese, and the variations among the standards of America's governing bodies are chiefly variations of wording: it is possible to get lost in verbiage, and then to realize that many of these standards really mean the same thing. There is virtually complete agreement as to what characteristics are desirable, and in South Africa, Australia and New Zealand, the British standard is used.

An important point emerges from the American standards: the excellent description under *Chin and jaw*. The Cat Fanciers Association, the American Cat Association and the Siamese Cat Society of America give under this heading: 'Tip of chin lines up with tip of nose in the same vertical plane. Neither receding nor excessively massive.' This is the best description of this feature which has so far appeared; its importance lies in the fact that if the desired length of head be carried to extreme, then a receding chin and weak lower jaw will result. This part of the Siamese standard gives an immediate mental picture of the lower half of a leonine profile—the well-shaped lower jaw of a healthy cat.

## CHANGES AND VARIATIONS

The alterations which have taken place in the type of the Siamese are the results of selective breeding carried out with the intention of producing individuals conforming to the approved standards. The first of these cats to come to Britain were slightly bigger than their present-day descendants and had heads that were much rounder, still, they were a small breed, and the heads had a certain length not present in British shorthairs. Some of them squinted, and some had kinks in their tails but all had long legs and a definite contrast between body-colour and points-colour. The committee which was concerned with them approved the length of head, the colour-contrast, the long-legged rather slender look and the narrow-shaped deep blue eyes; it did not favour the squint nor the malformed tails. It drew up a standard accordingly, and breeders have ever since done their best to conform to it. If they wanted to win prizes they had to breed in accordance with the standard by which the judges would make decisions and, in any case, there was general agreement as to what would constitute a beautiful specimen of the breed.

The method used was the only one possible: to mate together two cats with characteristics which approximated as nearly as possible to the requirements of the standard. No knowledge of the science of heredity is needed to suggest this way of breeding for it is simply commonsense; everyone knows, without being told, that creatures tend to resemble their ancestors. Although there were necessarily some setbacks, breeders have, by-and-large, achieved their aims, and have produced some extraordinarily beautiful cats. If it were possible for us to set side-by-side the best Siamese of the 1906 Crystal Palace exhibition of cats and the best-in-show Siamese of, say, the Siamese Cat Club's most recent show, we should be surprised at the difference between them. It is certain that the cat of today would have a markedly longer head; and he would probably be finer-boned more svelte and with, very possibly, more delicate texture of coat and a longer tail. We ought, in the interests of health, to be careful not to overdo the length of head; as suggested in the American standards, excessive length of head leads to chinlessness, and it is a danger signal, not only because a firm chin is attractive to look at, but because of the inevitable weakening of the lower jaw; to breed for the long, straight profile which nowadays wins prizes may produce a very weak lower jaw and may look wonderful in profile but 'pinched' when seen full-face; one of our most experienced Siamese judges has said 'The poor creatures won't be able to eat soon'; and it is much to be hoped that breeders will see the red light and try for the firm wedge head which means health rather than for the exaggeratedly long one which could spoil the lovely heads. We have, however, probably made the very best of these beautiful creatures, and the changes have brought out the most attractive features of the breed.

## CHOCOLATE-POINTS

Even more striking than the alterations in type are the different points-colours which have appeared. The first to be observed was probably chocolate. I have a coloured picture of a chocolate-pointed Siamese called Banshee who was bred in the early years of this century. The picture was given to me in the late 1950's by Mrs French, who had bred Banshee. A curious fact about the picture of this cat is that her type is far better, judging by our present standard, than that of many of the early champions, whose pictures show cats with wonderful colour-contrast but, very often, round, plump-cheeked faces. This little chocolate-pointed of early days was a good example of the changes which have taken place in type, and a pioneer of the true wedge heads. Mrs French and her friend Miss Fitzwilliam thought highly of the chocolate-coloured points, but their opinion was not shared by other fanciers, who said that these cats were 'just bad "seals" '. In consequence, the chocolate-pointed kittens were neutered whenever they appeared. They came into their own after the second world war. In 1948 the late B. A. Stirling-Webb, one of the great experimental breeders and who had, of course, known Banshee, wrote in the Siamese Cat Club *News Sheet* that he could discover only 13 chocolate-pointed cats alive at that date. He was Britain's foremost experimental breeder; it was he who established the colour-points (see p. 26, and called Himalayans in America) with their wonderful long pelage and fine type—and all from a little female called Georgie who was a Siamese with long fur. He also, with a few interested breeders, established rex-coated cats, first bred by Mrs Ennismore and discovered as recently as 1956 by Dr A. G. Searle and the late A. C. Jude, in Cornwall. The researches that Mr Stirling-Webb made were carefully carried out and are absolutely reliable; he found that nine of the existing chocolate-pointeds were descended from a cat called 'Litabois', a seal-point born in 1918, who was a great-grandson of 'Prince of Siam', imported in 1897.

It is easy to understand the general admiration for the seal-points; the contrast between the creamy coat and the dark, dense points of a really good specimen of this variety is extremely beautiful. Indeed, it is probable that if an opinion poll could be taken as to the preferences of Siamese cat lovers for this or that points colour, the seal-points would easily top the list. However, the other colours also have their votaries, and both Mrs French and Miss Wentworth Fitzwilliam lived to come to the inaugural meeting of the Chocolate-pointed Cat Club. The 'chocolates' were recognized and their standard approved by the Governing Council. By the time they obtained recognition, genetics was beginning to be understood, and people knew that the colour did not represent 'bad "seal"', but was a brown dilution of eumelanin, the gene for which is recessive to seal.

### BLUE-POINTS

Meanwhile, long before the chocolate-points were seen in the show pens, the blue-pointeds had made their appearance. Since some of the cats originally imported from Siam had the necessary genotype inherited from their forebears of long ago, probably the self-blue cats of Malaya, this colour was bound, sooner or later, to appear in the phenotype: a mating took place between cats both carrying the gene for blue dilution of eumelanin, and a blue-pointed kitten was born. It has to be remembered that although blue, in the coat-colour of cats, is a straightforward Mendelian recessive which will give a 1 in 4 ratio of blues to seals when it is carried by both parents, this does not mean that every fourth kitten from such a mating will be a blue; there might be a couple of litters of only seals or a whole litter of blues; over a number of similar matings it will be found that one-in four kittens are blue-pointed.

This variety also had its admirers and its detractors. The thriving Blue-pointed Siamese Cat Club was founded by Mrs Duncan Hindley in 1944. We owe a great deal not only to our experimental breeders and the enormous amount of work that they do, but also to those who, like Mrs Hindley, are sufficiently liberal-minded to champion what is new and attractive, often against the tide of popular opinion.

The perfect blue-point has points the colour of a thistle-stalk, and a truly glacial white coat; it is an exquisite colour-combination. For this variety also B. A. Stirling-Webb's researches are of value. Writing in 1949, again in the Siamese Cat Club's *News Sheet,* he tells us that he expected to find records of early importations of blue-pointeds, but discovered only one: there was a Lady Blue Blue of Pegu in the first volume of the Siamese Cat Club Register; he quotes from *Our Cats and all about Them* by C. A. House: 'At the Holland House show of 1896, Mr Spearman, a young Englishman just home from Siam, exhibited a blue Siamese. The cat was blue instead of biscuit colour, as were the majority of Siamese which we had seen up to that time, and Mr Louis Wain, who was judging, refused to recognise it as a Siamese and left it out. He argued with Mr Spearman that it was not a Siamese, but that gentleman said it was and that there were others in Siam from where he had previously bought it.' Mr Stirling-Webb goes on: 'From the above it is not quite clear whether this was a blue-pointed or a blue-all-over cat . . . the question arises whether it was not a Korat cat, which was an all-blue shorthair recognised in Siam.' However, he tells us that the earliest cat known to be a blue-pointed mentioned in the Siamese Cat Club register was Rhoda, born in 1894.

### LILAC-POINTS

Once the 'chocolates' and the 'blues' had been approved and accepted, geneticists were not slow to suggest to their friends in the fancy that lilac might be produced in the points of a Siamese. I have a letter from the late A. C. Jude in which he writes, '. . . I wonder someone does not try for a lilac. . . .' In fact, the first lilac-pointed Siamese were bred by the introduction of Russian Blue, and the first kitten born from Siamese lineage only was of my breeding. To breed a lilac-pointed Siamese it is necessary for genes for blue and brown (chocolate) to be present in both parents. 'The lilac point is a dilute chocolate point.'[1] Gene action is extremely complex; the melanocyte, migrating successfully from the neural crest, will produce pigment granules, and the colour seen in the phenotype depends, among many other things, upon the shape, numbers and arrangement of these melanin granules. However, once a lilac-pointed cat has been achieved, he will breed true: lilac to lilac will produce only lilac.

The colour of the points of these cats is almost impossible to describe. In the best cats the points are the palest imaginable beige with a rosy tinge which, in fact, gives a faint suggestion of pink lilac. The faults to beware of are blue in the points of this variety, or a decidedly yellow colour which now and then appears and which is enough to spoil any lilac-pointed cat. It is important to realise that this yellow has no connection with phaeomelanin and is not the same thing at all as the yellow of red cats and cream cats; it is, in fact, a sort of dilution of eumelanin; we see rather more often than we want to, if we are breeders, judges or exhibitors, fawn in the coats of the blue-pointeds, and sometimes a merging into a reddish shade at the edges of the points of a 'seal'. All these are dilutions of melanin, including the undesireable yellow occasionally found in the points of a 'lilac', which derives quite simply from a lack of intensity in the chocolate pigment. Remembering that this very beautiful lilac colour is made up of blue and the extremely volatile chocolate, it is easy to understand that there can sometimes be either too much blue to be seen, or the yellowing that comes of dilute chocolate. In fact, it is agreeable to know that not very many of the cats of this variety exhibit either fault; most have the rosy, pale-beige tint of the true lilac. This is a good example of the help that breeders derive from knowing the genotype of their cats.

The 'chocolates' and the 'lilacs' have a peculiar advantage over the other colours in one respect: their coats are much more likely to be pale. The eumelanin granules for brown are spheroid rather than oval as in black (seal), and the colour which they produce is volatile. This has the disadvantages of its merits; the masks and other points of the chocolate-pointed and lilac-pointed cats often remain incomplete for much longer than is the case with the seal-points or blue-points; you can find a chocolate-pointed cat of a year old whose mask is still incomplete. To offset this, many a seal-or blue-point is spoilt by the spreading of colour to the coat, sometimes to a sufficient extent to ruin the cat's appearance; whereas the fly-away brown or lilac seldom if ever covers the coat and, indeed, many of the cats live to be old without the slightest shading on their bodies. 'Mine never got darker with age as the seal-pointeds generally do. Their coats are similar in texture and the points should be a rich café-au-lait.'[2]

Chapter three

# Standards, changes and variations: II

## RED-POINTS

While the lilac-pointed cats were first under consideration two ladies, Dr Norah Archer in Britain and Mrs da Felippo in America, were working towards the production of red-pointed Siamese. Their success in this was important and far-reaching. It was the first time a new colour had been introduced into Siamese since they acquired a gene for blue possibly tens of thousands of years ago; the results have been of great interest, and were probably not foreseen by the average fancier.

The experimental breeder works harder and spends more money than is generally realised; in dealing with any new factor or factors it is necessary to house, feed, care for and find homes for many kittens not directly required for the work in hand. Bills for food, housing, vaccination and, if you have any ill-luck, veterinary attention, can be enormous; keeping the cattery clean and its occupants properly waited-on is time-consuming; and a great deal of thought has to be given to the placing of kittens, possibly with people who wish to join in the experiment, perhaps as neutered pets in good homes. Since the kittens which are to become pets cannot properly be said to be of pedigree stock, they must be given away, and the breeder has the anxiety of making sure that they go to really good homes. Those who undertake such work are usually dedicated to it, and their reward is the successful breeding of a beautiful creature.

Yellow, in mammals, comes from phaeomelanin which, unlike eumelanin, is soluble, but whose chemical processes are as yet (1969) imperfectly understood; various theories have been advanced by biochemists of note to account for the switch from eumelanin to phaeomelanin which takes place, presumably, in the melanocyte; it is possible that this is accomplished by one of the aminoacids. But we have to await a definite scientific pronouncement. We know that phaeomelanin is responsible for the light bands in the agouti hairs of the tabby, and that its presence is required for the yellow of the points of the red-pointed Siamese; but this is not of great importance to the breeders. Very important indeed with regard to this variety is the fact that yellow, in the cat, is sex-linked. This has already been extensively discussed and written about; but it is a matter of such moment to breeders of red-pointeds that it is worth while to give here a brief outline of the gene action concerned.

Chromosomes exist in pairs, and are the vehicles upon which the genes are carried. Cell division takes place and the gametes, the ova and the spermatozoa, carry, each, one of every chromosome pair. In the case of the X and the Y, the sex-determining chromosomes, each ovum carries an X and each spermatozoon carries either an X or a Y. At fertilization the pairs of chromosomes are restored, so that the new zygote (in the case under discussion the new Siamese kitten) receives its diploid number—its full complement of chromosomes—half from its sire and half from its dam. In the case of the sex chromosome, it gets from its dam an X, and from its sire either an X or a Y. If the new combination is XX, the kitten is a female, if it is XY, the new kitten is a male. The chances of there being a boy or a girl are equal; as you could toss a handful of coins a few times and find they would, overall, come down in equality as to heads or tails, so the ova, necessarily carrying X, stand a fifty-fifty chance of being fertilized by a sperm carrying X or one carrying Y.

The genes, for which the chromosomes are the vehicles, also exist in pairs, and for them also the pairs, separated at cell-division and carried in linear order on the chromosomes, are restored at fertilization. It is gene action which governs the characters evident in an individual, and a gene carried on the sex-determining chromosome is said to be 'sex-linked'. In the cat, the gene for yellow is sex-linked; it is carried on the X chromosome and not on the Y and, in addition, yellow is dominant in the male kittens, and incompletely dominant in the female kittens. If a yellow (red, ginger, marmalade) male be mated to a black female the male kittens will all be black, because they will have received an X from their black dam, and a Y, not carrying yellow, from their sire. The female kittens will all be tortoiseshells because they will have from their sire an X, carrying yellow which, in the female kittens is partially dominant.

Thus:

| | | | | |
|---|---|---|---|---|
| Black female | ● | X | ○ | Yellow male |
| Genes | ●......................................................○ | | | Genes |
| for | ●......................................................○ | | | for yellow |
| Black | ●......................................................○ | | | carried only |
| | ●......................................................○ | | | on X |

● Black male ⊙ Tortie female ● Black male ⊙ Tortie female

If, however, a yellow female be mated to a black male, the situation is different; their sons will all be yellow, having received an X, carrying yellow dominant in the male kittens from their yellow dam; and the daughters, with an X carrying a gene for yellow incompletely dominant in the female kittens will, once again, be tortoiseshells.

So:

| | | | | |
|---|---|---|---|---|
| Yellow female | ○ | X | ● | Black male |
| Genes for yellow | | | | |
| dominant in | ○......................................................● | | | Genes |
| male kittens, | ○......................................................● | | | for |
| incompletely so | ○......................................................● | | | black |
| in female | ○......................................................● | | | |

○ Yellow male ⊙ Tortie female ○ Yellow male ⊙ Tortie female

The foregoing diagrams will show, to anyone not already conversant with it, the peculiar behaviour of yellow in the cat. Those pioneers who set out to breed red-points began with a Siamese and a red tabby; a self-red, showing no tabby markings would have been ideal, but such cats are extremely rare. Years ago I saw two, in a garden as I passed by; they appeared to be adults and to have no tabby markings. Since then I have asked myself whether they were, in fact, big kittens who would develop the tabby pattern later; for tabby is the original wild-type, and appears more often than one might think; there are even 'ghost' tabby markings on some Siamese coats, and there are many Siamese with tabby rings on their tails; and most people have seen the shorthair black cat on whose coat stripes are visible in a clear light. So, with a Siamese, complete with the factor for restriction of colour to the points, and with the desired long, graceful, foreign type, and a sturdy, thoroughly British-type red tabby, the behaviour of the gene for whose coat-colour was, to say the least, unusual, this experiment was begun. It has produced one of the most beautiful Siamese cats ever seen in a show-pen.

If a red male be mated to a seal-pointed female, a red-pointed male may appear in the second family (F2) thus:

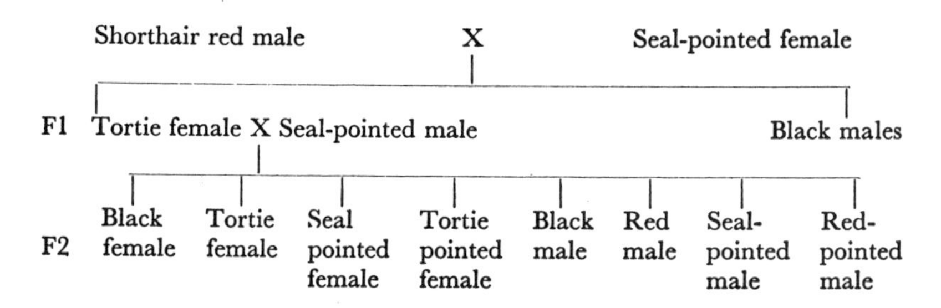


If a red female be used, the possibilities are wider:

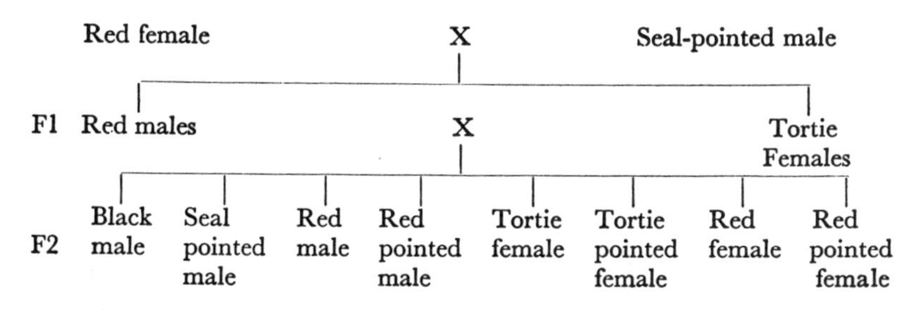


#### STANDARD FOR RED-POINTED COLOUR

The British standard for the red-pointed Siamese (1976) as drawn up by the club which caters for them and approved by the Governing Council gives for their colour:

*Body*: White, shading (if any) to be apricot on the back. Kittens paler.
*Nose leather*: Pink.
*Ears*: Bright reddish gold.
*Mask*: Bright reddish gold.
*Legs and feet*: Bright reddish gold or apricot.
*Tail*: Bright reddish gold.
*Eyes*: Bright vivid blue.
*Modification*: Barring or striping on mask, legs or tail is not to be deemed a fault.

The bright reddish gold asked for under colour is extremely beautiful; it is not, curiously enough, the shade considered best for red tabbies. For red tabbies the markings, as set forth in their standard, should be 'Very dense, and dark red . . . ground colour and markings to be as rich red as possible'. And for longhair red tabbies the standard asks for 'Deep rich red colour'. I recently asked one of the officers of the Red-pointed Siamese Cat Club, Mrs Pring, for the club's views on the shade desired for the red-pointeds; and she agreed that the bright reddish gold of the points of these cats is not the same as the dark colour of the best red tabbies; she said that there might, in due time, be a modification of the colour and a consequent alteration of the standard. From the artistic point of view there is, however, a lot to be said for the present bright gold.

The standard for colour in cream-pointed Siamese, which are of course the dilute of red, and which were recognized by the Council in 1976, reads:

*Body*: White, shading (if any) to palest cream.
*Nose leather*: Pink.
*Mask*: Cream, with tracings to ears, except in kittens.
*Ears, legs and feet*: Cream.
*Tail*: Cream.
*Eyes*: Bright vivid blue.
*Modification*: Barring and striping on mask, legs and tail is *not* to be deemed a serious fault. Note: a hot cream is not desirable.

A point of interest in the Siamese standards in America concerns the red-points, cream-points and all Siamese cats heterozygous for yellow. Genetically, a cat with red points is a Siamese in the same sense as is the blue-point. The red has been introduced from a red tabby or a self-red, just as the blue was introduced by a blue-all-over cat, probably in Malaya. But these cats are not always recognised in America as Siamese. In fact, in any country, the recognition of what is new always takes time. In America, the fault found with red-pointeds has been that they are hybrids. Years ago, the dictionary meaning of hybrid was given as a cross between two species. The word came to us through the Latin *hybrida,* from the Greek *hubris*, which means a sort of pride; and through the centuries it came to denote distortion or damage. In *Webster's International Dictionary* and the *Oxford Dictionary* however, hybrid is, now, given as a cross between two varieties, and has become a word used to denote heterogeneity. We have come a long way from *hubris*; and hybrid today, used in its adjectival sense, means heterozygous. Therefore it has lost, or ought to have lost, the derogatory meaning that it had in the days when it denoted the result of a cross between two *species*: such a cross would produce an infertile animal, as a mule, for example, which is a cross between horse and ass, and would be, by-and-large, undesirable. But for an animal to be heterozygous *within* a species is not undesirable at all; it may even be a splendid thing, bringing new health to an inbred, weakened variety. Although the red-pointeds in America are not at present recognised as Siamese, there are standards for them, and they can be shown. The Cat Fanciers Association calls these cats red colourpoint shorthairs; the Crown Cat Fanciers Federation lists them under 'Siamese'; the American Cat Association calls red-points and tortie-points 'colourpoints'; and some of the American standards give tabby-points and tortie-points of all colours as 'exotics'. The Cat Fanciers Association starts with the statement 'The red colourpoint shorthair is a separate breed'.

There are further differences between the British and the American standards. In America the eyes of all Siamese are desired to be of a deep blue, whereas the British standard demands this depth of eye-colour for the seal-points and tortie-points, but for the other colours has 'vivid blue'. It has always been considered in Britain that the eye-colour of, for example, blue-points, had less intense sapphire depth than those of the seal-pointeds, but there have appeared blue-points with really deeply blue eyes, and this is what is aimed at in the American standards. In Australia the same question has recently arisen as has been discussed in Britain: does the standard err in describing eye-colour in blue-pointeds as 'china blue'? This has been altered in Britain to 'clear, bright, vivid blue'; and it seems possible that the new description allows too much latitude for the individual preference of the judge; some may prefer that the eye-colour for this variety, while it must never be pale, should be less deeply blue than that for seal-points; while others may like to see, as sometimes happens, a blue-point with the dark, sapphire eye-colour present in the best seal-points. It could be argued that bright, vivid blue describes either shade; but it may be that opinion in both Australia and Britain is in favour of there being no great difference of eye-colour for these varieties. Such questions will doubtless resolve themselves in due time in a land where so many clubs and societies cater for the breed.

Strange to English people is the Crown Cat Fanciers Federation's standard for the blue-pointeds, which reads 'Body colour should be an even platinum grey of bluish tone . . . '. To those accustomed to look for 'glacial white' in the coats of cats of this variety, this does indeed read strangely. But whereas a blue-point who has recently died at the age of 16½ years had a white coat to the last, there have been of late years far too many blue-points showing fawn in their coats. The American standards stress the undesirability of this, and the American Cat Association has for these cats 'Body, bluish-white'. The standards in the United States do not, if you examine them carefully, differ very much in essentials either from each other or from the European standards. If strictly adhered to, they will produce very beautiful cats.

The question of barring on legs or tail in the red-points is very difficult to resolve. Plainly a self-red would have no tabby pattern at all; however, these are rare in Britain, although Madame Hollenstein, Switzerland's foremost international judge, tells me there are beautiful self-reds in Scandinavia. In Britain, red tabbies must have been used in the original breeding of red-points; and all the cats that ever there were came originally from the tabby wild-type; since even the seal-pointeds occasionally show faint tabby 'ghost' patterns, it is unlikely that red-points—or for the matter of that lilac-points—will often appear with no barring at all.

One of the difficulties for breeders of this variety of Siamese cat has been the fairly frequent absence of colour on their legs and paws; you can sometimes come across an otherwise excellent specimen whose gloves and boots are much too pale or even, though more rarely, absent; this situation seems to tend to right itself to a greater or lesser extent as the cat becomes older. The question of shading is important but a great many of these cats have none; and so many have been bred with truly fine type and colouring, notably in New Zealand, and have won not only championships but best-in-show awards that it is obviously possible to overcome any show faults in them. They will, moreover, have gained in health and stamina from the cross necessarily made with the good strong red tabby.

'Nothing could be better than a small, inbreeding community, provided the original genes are healthy'.[1] As matters stand, it is the last six words which make the operative phrase. There is no doubt that some Siamese have in days gone by carried lethal genes; breeders who, nowadays, are more alive to the danger than were their predecessors, have to a great extent righted the trouble by neutering any suspects. Lethality is difficult to trace to its source; it is, for instance, possible for there to be in an organism gains or losses of

7 Champion female tabby-point "Robseane Lynx Tyli", bred by Dr and Mrs J C Fanning and owned by Mr and Mrs Slocombe, all of Adelaide, Australia

8 Grand Champion "Ophir's Black Opal", seal-point owned and bred by Harry and Mary Lou Nolan of Atlanta, Georgia, USA

9 Champion tabby-point "San-T-Ree Filigree", owned by Kristina Erblad of Göteborg, Sweden

10 Tabby-point kitten "Warana Silver Talisman", bred by Mary Batten of Brisbane, Australia

11 Tabby-point kitten "Vaillencourt Solomon", belonging to Mr and Mrs M Elliott of Erith, Kent, England

12 Tabby-point queen "Spotlight Muscatel" with litter of tabby and seal-points.
Owner: Mrs S Smith of Thurleigh, Bedfordshire, England

13 Seal-point owned by Mrs W A Wawrukiewicz of San Francisco, California, USA

14 Chocolate tabby-point "Eileen de la Fuente", bred by M Henchoz and owned by Mme. Walther de Bons of Domdidier, Switzerland

15 Tabby-point kitten "Whiterose Tia-Maria", owned by Mrs S Smith of Thurleigh, Bedfordshire, England

16 Chocolate-point "Pentangle Beadman", owned by Mrs P Moss of Rushden, Northamptonshire, England

small sections of chromosomes. This produces a chromosomal imbalance and will probably have no particular effect in the heterozygote, but it is lethal in the homozygote. So, in Siamese cats, inbreeding, perhaps a backcross, may bring together two individuals who have a similar chromosomal imbalance, and some or all of the kittens will die. They may be born seeming perfectly healthy—no one will know why they did not survive. But this is a probable cause. Any genetic imbalance is bad, and it will be perpetuated by inbreeding; the reason for 'fading' kittens has not been found, but they may die because of such an imbalance. It is a warning.

A certain fragility, a certain stupidity even, comes to closely inbred organisms. This has happened in the case of European royal houses; it happened in days gone by in little village communities where incest was common; it has ruined some breeds of dogs; it will lead eventually to sterility and death of a breed. There is no doubt that the introduction of good, strong tabby genes into these cats, bred as they are from comparatively few imported individuals, will do no harm at all and will probably do much good.

Of course, the breeding programmes designed by fanciers lead to an end-product which can be and very often is produced in communities of free-living cats. Years ago Miss Dukes, a member of the committee of the Siamese Cat Association, found such a cat, and he became part of Dr Norah Archer's breeding programme for the production of red-pointeds. He was 'Somerville Scarlet Pimpernel', son of a seal-point sire called 'Yew Tree Yanto' and, obviously, a shorthair red queen. Miss Dukes describes him as having points definitely darker than the rest of his coat. From the point of view of show quality man, as a selective agent, does a far more sophisticated job than would be achieved by haphazard matings. A cat whose parents have been carefully chosen, whose food is of the best, who is regularly groomed and always provided with warmth and with fresh air is likely to produce kittens with a sleekness, an appearance approximating to the show standard, and an air of being an 'aristocat' not found in an ordinary 'moggie', however well-loved.

Any new variety of cat brought forward comes under the fire of criticism by the cat fancy. This is as it should be, for if everything new were instantly accepted, many mistakes would be made. A fresh breed or variety is usually sponsored by a club, exhibited by breeders 'for exhibition only', that is, not for competition, and brought by the club to the notice of the Governing Council. As discussed in Chapter

9, the relevant Council rule demands that the kitten have three generations of like breeding behind it: the kitten brought forward for the Council's attention, its parents, grandparents and great-grandparents all to be of the same breed or variety. This sounds very strict and at first glance some may think it unnecessary; but without such precautions a few cats not previously seen might be shown, judged, sold for breeding, and then found to be the only ones of their kind: no like ancestry, no certainty of like progeny, nothing really new about the pattern—just a come-by-chance difference; the breeders, the sponsoring club, the Council would all look ridiculous, and there would be disappointment for those who had been interested. As things are, anything new is kept waiting for recognition, but when the Council does recognise it and grant a standard, the newcomer is very firmly established indeed.

While he is waiting for recognition, the new cat is discussed, argued about, praised and denigrated; this is criticism and often valuable, for exchange of ideas can be very useful. If the new mutation is of value it will in due course receive recognition. In the early days, one of the accusations levelled against red-pointeds was that they were hybrids. Let it be said at once that they are not hybrids in the old sense of the term; as stated above, a mule was a hybrid, being a cross between two different animals; in the new sense, hybrid is given as a heterozygote. In neither sense will hybrid do for a red-pointed Siamese: Siamese cats and red cats are of the same species, and all living things are heterozygous for some character or other. However, it was said that these were not in fact Siamese. As to this, it would seem to be important to define a Siamese cat. If by 'Siamese cat' you mean a cat whose ancestry stems entirely from Siam, then no cat carrying any other ancestry will conform with the definition. It has, however, generally been accepted though not, I believe, stated in any rule, that the definition of a Siamese cat is 'a cat whose eyes are blue and whose coat-pattern is governed in the phenotype by the factors for restriction-of-colour-to-points'. It is also accepted that a cat is judged by its appearance 'on the day'; and it is possible to exhibit a Siamese cat with a *known* far-off tabby ancestor —and to win with him. It may be noted that such a cat will breed true; mated to his like he will, since both are recessive to full colour, produce only his like. Mated to tabby, he would produce tabby kittens even if he were himself 'pure' for Siamese, since full colour is the dominant.

There are in fact plenty of Siamese of great beauty and conformity to type who have a bend-sinister somewhere; Siamese cats have been in the west a long time, and even in the case of individuals whose known ancestry for numerous generations is 'pure' for the breed, we cannot be sure that there is no cat of full colour far, far back in their pedigrees, particularly since we have it on good authority that the common-or-garden feline in Siam is, as with us, the tabby. Individuals and Committees all over the world have argued whether red-points ought or ought not to compete for top honours at shows, the case against them being that they are not true Siamese. Whether a red-pointed is a true Siamese or not will depend upon whether you accept that a Siamese cat is, by definition, a short-haired blue-eyed cat whose colour is restricted to the points. If you do accept this definition, then the red-pointeds are Siamese. But if you do not accept it, you come up against a difficulty: the blue-points and chocolate-pointeds came originally from crosses with cats respectively blue all over and brown all over; the factors for blue and brown dilution of melanin came into play, and the 'blues' and 'chocolates' are recognised as Siamese. But, if their remote ancestors were self-blues and self-browns, then they are no less and no more 'hybrids' than the red-points, whose points colour comes from a red-all-over cat. Nature can and will produce red-points unaided by fanciers; madam from Siam will meet a fine ginger tom in the garden; her kind owner will keep one of her kits—a pretty little tortie, maybe, and mate her to the Siamese stud—and lo and behold, one of her kittens will be a male red-pointed. No matter what man approves, nature will see that unusual coat-patterns appear; in this case she has produced a red cat whose colour shows only in the points; it is the fancier who has seen to it that his line should be carried on in such a manner as to give his progeny the lovely Siamese type. In most countries now, the idea that a red-pointed is 'not a Siamese' must seem as strange as would the notion, put forward years ago, that the blue-pointeds were 'wishy-washy'!

### TORTOISESHELL-POINTS

The tortoiseshell-pointed cats are very interesting; exactly as with the full tortoiseshells, they are to all intents and purposes always females. It will not do to say that no tortoiseshell male was ever born, since people of repute have said that they have seen them, although such cats are always sterile. This is curious, and stems from the peculiar behaviour of yellow in the coat-colour of the cat; for if a red female be mated with a male of any other colour, her sons, receiving from her an X chromosome carrying yellow dominant in the male offspring, should all be red. If one turns up who is a tortoiseshell like his sisters then he is an oddity. The best theory so far put forward to account for such individuals is that which postulates a kitten with two X chromosomes, as well as a Y. This would constitute a genic imbalance—a state of affairs which usually spells trouble. In face of such an imbalance, it seems that the kitten concerned is fortunate if the only results are sterility and the wearing of a tortoiseshell suit—or tortoiseshell points.

The little tortoiseshell females are, in fact, a step towards the red-pointed cats; they are the daughters of one red parent, and the potential dams of red-point litters comprising both males and females. When, however, you have a really well-marked tortie-point, she will be very attractive to look at, and a standard for these cats has been approved, just as one was accepted for the tortoiseshells. For colour this standard gives:

*Colour*: Restricted to points as in all Siamese; basic colour seal, blue, chocolate or lilac.

*Body*: As in equivalent solid colour Siamese.

*Nose leather*: As in equivalent solid colour Siamese.

*Mask*: Seal, blue, chocolate or lilac patched or mingled with red and/or cream.

*Ears*: Basic colours as in mask, patched or mingled with red and/or cream.

*Note*: Distribution of patching on points-colour and leathers of all tortie-point Siamese is random and immaterial. Barring and ticking shall be deemed a fault.

It would have been very difficult not to give recognition to these cats, for their markings, like those of the full tortoiseshells, have a quaint charm of their own; some have a blaze, often a red blaze, making them look like the Norman men-at-arms in the Bayeux tapestry; many have remarkably even markings, and make good show specimens; and most have a look of the Commedia del Arte, making it easy to understand why Dr Norah Archer called one of hers 'Harlequina'. Although the torties and tortie-pointeds are, by reason of their sex-linked yellow, virtually always females, so that they cannot ever constitute a family with four generations of like breeding, yet it is proper that standards should have been granted to them; for they will, whenever a line of cats carries genes for yellow, always be both useful and decorative: the torties are the 'coloured cats' of the English countryside and tortie-points are the natural outcome of the introduction of yellow into Siamese.

### TABBY-POINTS

Before the red-points were recognized, however, a new variety came upon the scene: the tabby-pointeds. At the Croydon Cat Club's championship show of 1961, Miss Alexander of Etchingham exhibited some kittens with Siamese type and 'stripey' points. These and similar kittens bred by Mrs Warner appeared at further shows, in Any Other Variety classes, of course, since they had no standard and so could not compete in championship classes—and they were very much admired and discussed. They were the tabby-points of today, although at first many names were suggested for them, including 'tiger-pointed', 'lynx-pointed' and 'shadow-pointed'. Tabby-point, which was finally chosen, is the best possible name for them, for it is both charming and factual.

These cats had a spectacular rise to fame and fortune. One of Miss Alexander's kittens was at once bought by Mrs Hindley (who was always able to see what is beautiful in a Siamese cat), and they were carefully fostered by her, by Mrs Warner and by other breeders. They had, almost from the word 'go', extraordinarily fine Siamese type, and in what seemed a very short time they were recognized and established, and were winning best-in-show awards. Their breeding brings out a point made by Dr Norah Archer: that so much Siamese breeding has been done in Britain that many a free cat population comprises individuals heterozygous for the restriction-of-colour-to-points factor, that is, carrying this factor. The kitten bought by Mrs Hindley in 1961 was called 'Tansy'; she was a tabby-pointed queen with very good type, the daughter of a seal-pointed queen called 'Patti', whose dam had 'got out' and mated with an unknown male, presumably a tabby. It is very unusual for a mis-mating to produce a Siamese of any sort; the fact that 'Patti' was a seal-pointed cat of good type shows quite clearly that the mate whom her dam found for herself was a cat who carried the gene for Siamese: he was probably a tabby from another free mating; 'Patti's' appearance on the scene makes it quite clear that the Siamese coat-pattern was on both sides of her family, and the fact that she subsequently produced a *whole litter* of tabby-pointed kittens indicates that her sire was a tabby cat carrying Siamese genes.

The standard for this variety gives the colouring as:

*General body colour*: Pale coat preferably free from body markings and conforming to recognized Siamese standard for the particular colour of points.

*Ears*: Solid, no stripes, thumb mark.

*Nose leather*: Conforming to recognized Siamese standard for the particular colour of points, or pink.

*Mask*: Clearly-defined stripes, especially round the eyes and nose. Distinct markings on cheeks, darkly spotted whisker pads.

*Eyes*: Brilliant clear blue. The lids dark-rimmed or toning with the points.

*Legs*: Varied sized broken stripes, solid markings on back of hind legs.

*Tail*: Varied sized clearly defined rings ending in a solid tip.

The thumb mark referred to is a patch on the ear for all the world as if it had been made by a thumb pressed into coloured ink and then onto the cat's ear. The description given in the standard is extraordinarily attractive, with its picture of eyes outlined in dark colour and dark spots on the whisker pads; and the cats exhibited have conformed to it splendidly, and shown outstanding Siamese type. It has to be remembered that these cats can be 'bred back' to seal-pointeds whenever the breeder desires; in this way the elegant type can be preserved, and the round-faced four-square 'British' look bred out; the cats, having attained their four generations of like breeding in the matter of Siamese coat-pattern, will breed true in this respect: a tabby point mated with a 'pure' seal-point will have only kittens with the Siamese coat-pattern. So far as the colour of the points is concerned, such a mating is a back-cross, i.e. the mating of a heterozygote to a homozygote; the heterozygote is the tabby-pointed, with mixed genes for tabby and for seal; and the seal is the homozygote—with only one colour. Being a back-cross, this will produce seal-points and tabby-points which will appear, over a number of matings, in equality. Extra Siamese type will thus be made available to the tabby-points, and also extra paleness for their coats. This last is very important, for the danger in breeding these cats lies in the fact that the wild-type tabby has a strong tendency to spread to the coat, so that you may find you have bred a tabby cat with Siamese type. It is therefore really advisable to cross tabby-points with seal-points now and then, to preserve both type and coat-colour.

This usefulness of an occasional back-cross applies also to the red-points, for no one wants a red tabby with Siamese type, and as with the tabby-points the fine type which has been produced will be preserved by such a cross, and is in fact being so preserved by well-known breeders. It is worth noting that the kittens from such a mating are all pedigree cats, for whom there should be no difficulty in finding good homes. The little tabby-points have one show advantage over other colours in Siamese: in the reds, lilacs—indeed in all the basic colours—stripes and ringed tails are a drawback; in the tabby-pointeds they are a necessity. Judge a 'seal' with some ghost markings on his flanks or a 'lilac' with rings on his tail, and a mark or so has to come off; but a 'tabby' depends upon his rings and his stripes to qualify for his class; so that the tabby pattern present in the genetic make-up of most cats, and not desired in some show cats, is actually right for the tabby-pointeds.

### SIAMESE IN EUROPE

There are very good show Siamese in Europe, where the British Standard is used. In 1977 at an extremely well-run show in Cologne sponsored by a new and very efficient club, Pro Kat, exhibits were present from many countries; Best-in-Show Siamese was a red-pointed of very high quality; the runner-up was a wonderful chocolate-pointed male, hard to fault, Cala Guya Papageno, who belongs, as I found after the show, to a Dutch lady who has for years exhibited Siamese of distinction. Standards for the cats derived from Siamese are very well understood in Europe; it was in Holland, long before Britain had a standard for them, that I first judged self-lilacs, according to the then provisional standard drawn up by a Dutch committee, and hardly different from the most recent British standard. Much later, in France, I saw in the home of their breeder, Mme M. C. Terrasse, a litter of kittens which comprised a really exquisite foreign lilac, Lancelot de Gravenoire. It was in Paris that I first saw an ebony. The cats derived from Siamese and self-shorthairs are the Havanas, foreign lilacs and foreign whites, for whom the Governing Council has approved standards; the 'foreign tabbies' with, as yet (1977), no official name; and the ebonies, so named in France. These are, in effect, Siamese cats with their colour not restricted to the points: the Havanas (chestnut brown) being the 'chocolates'. They have come about from matings with the various shorthairs, and the Siamese type has been wonderfully preserved. In Switzerland only the very best cats have been used for Siamese breeding, and in Scandinavia the red-pointeds have, more often than elsewhere, points nearing completion. Siamese are very well appreciated by the European breeders, and those who gain top honours at shows are exquisite creatures conforming extremely well to their standards.

### OTHER DILUTIONS

The production of red-points and then of tabby-points was more like a major-breakthrough than was generally realized at the time. Some fanciers no doubt foresaw the probabilities. In an article in *Our Cats* in 1962 I wrote: 'There is of course no reason in the world why Siamese cats should not be bred with points of any colour or permutation of colours proper to *felis domesticus*. . . .' But I have to confess I was simply making a statement of fact, and did not realise what was going to happen, nor give the matter much thought. However, the new colours appeared; there was a positive outburst of fresh patterns in the points of the cats, some come-by-chance, others intentionally produced, some foreseen by their breeders and quite a few turning up as complete surprises.

In 1968 a conference on new colours and patterns in Siamese cats was held at the Zoological Society of London's meeting rooms. At this conference proposals were made for the registration and show classification of Siamese cats, and these were occasioned by the new colours and patterns which had appeared in the points of the cats. The suggested classification began with self-pointed Siamese, i.e., the 'seals', 'blues', 'chocolates', lilacs' and 'reds' which were already recognized by the Council, and it included cream-points. The next suggested class was for tortie-points, the third for tabby-points and a fourth was for that rather baffling creature the tabby-tortie-point. There was at this conference an exhibition of cats, so that those who attended could see for themselves the multiplicity of new patterns which have evolved since the red-points and the tabby-points were bred, and one of these was a tabby-tortie-pointed cat: it was mentioned in the schedule for the exhibition that a tabby-tortie-point carrying blue and chocolate mated to a seal-point carrying blue and chocolate could produce all known colours and patterns of Siamese.

Of course, a tabby can be crossed with a blue, chocolate or lilac-point, and can thus produce, in the second family, kittens which are blue, chocolate or lilac-tabby-points. These constitute a definite series, easily recognizable for what they are. Mrs Clarke, a British judge who goes in for experimental breeding, has bred some blue-tabby-points of great beauty from silver tabbies. It is naturally perfectly possible to cross a brown tabby with Siamese, and it may be because of such a cross that there appear in the show-pens now and then cats which look like seal-tabby-points at one end, and like brown-tabby-points at the other end! It is interesting that Mrs Clarke has found that the tabby striations appear almost at once on the points of seal and blue-points, not until three months on chocolate-points, and as late as four months in the case of lilac-points. It thus seems that the pattern of stripes follows the basic colour—so firm in the 'seals' and 'blues', so volatile in the 'chocolates' and 'lilacs'. A chocolate-pointed kitten has often only the ghost of a mask at three months, so it is not surprising that the stripes of a chocolate-tabby-point should only just have appeared at that age.

The Governing Council, in its Standard of Points of September 1976, has approved the following standard for tortie-tabby points: As tabby-pointed with the following exceptions:
*Ears*: Mottled.
*Nose and pad leathers*: Mottled.
*Tail*: As tabby-pointed but mottling permissible.
*Points*: Patched with red and/or cream over tabby pattern. Distribution of patching on points immaterial (as in standard for tortie-points).
*Note*: These cats usually resemble tabby-points rather than tortie-points.
The scale of points for the tortie-tabby-points is given as:

| | |
|---|---|
| *Type and shape* | |
| As for seal-pointed Siamese | 50 |
| *Colour and Condition* | |
| Ringed tail | 10 |
| Eyes | 10 |
| Body colour | 15 |
| Points and thumb marks | 10 |
| Texture of coat and general condition | 5 |
| | 100 |

These, then, constitute the tabby-point series; it has been suggested that it ought to include red-tabby-points and cream-tabby-points—but here it seems possible to get into very deep waters; for many of the red-points were bred originally from red tabbies and not from the rare self-reds; the breeders' objective has been to breed out the stripes; it seems possible that to cross a red-point of quality with a tabby, brown or silver, might be a mistake.

The second series of new points patterns is, of course, the tortoiseshell series; and 'genetically the term tortoiseshell includes all cats heterozygous for yellow including blue-creams'.[2] It should be noted that the cat of either sex whose phenotype shows a yellow coat of whatever shade from dark red to pale cream is homozygous for O. The heterozygote is the cat—invariably female—who carries genes for yellow *and* other colours; remembering always that O is carried on the X chromosome only, and is dominant in the male kittens. So that any male carrying yellow must be yellow, and cannot possibly be a heterozygote in respect of coat-colour. There are two points worth remembering about that very awkward colour, yellow: first, whereas a fancier will talk of a red-pointed cat and a cream-pointed cat, to the geneticist both these are indicated by the symbol O, which stands for orange, and which was fairly recently substituted for Y for yellow by a nomenclature committee. Secondly, it is, from the fancier's angle, a tricky colour, the gene for which can produce unusual—and from the show point of view tiresome—variants; for instance, a blue-cream-pointed cat is the dilute of a tortie-pointed cat: the 'tortie' has points of intermingled black and red; the blue-cream-pointed has intermingled blue and cream; blue being a dilution of black, and cream a dilution of red. It is not quite so simple as it sounds; a 'tortie' can have cream as well as red, and there can be a blue-cream-pointed cat whose colouring comprises red as well as cream. You see little speckles of red as well as small cream patches in the blue points. Such a female may produce red-pointed kittens and cream-points; she may have kittens whose points are not of the desired shade for either variety—perhaps some may have points reminiscent of both oranges *and* lemons! The experienced breeder, of course, sets matters to rights in the time-honoured way—the only way—by selective breeding; in this case, by careful choice of a mate for the queen who is a dilute tortoiseshell showing red as well as its cream dilution in her points, and keeping the best kitten to breed from.

### BLUE, CHOCOLATE AND LILAC-TORTIE-POINTS

To return to the 'tortie' series, it is like the one for the tabby-points. Matings have taken place between red-pointeds and cats of other points colours, so that we have blue, chocolate and lilac-tortie-pointed cats. These are unusual and interesting, and they present no difficulties to breeder or judge: they are clearly recognizable, and a good specimen is quaint and charming, and conforms to the standard, with blue, chocolate or lilac as a basic colour instead of seal. It is interesting that the colouring extends to the paw-leather: look under the feet of a tortie-point, and where the foot is seal, the paw-pads will be black; if the foot is red, the paw-pads are pink—even to the extent of broken colouring on the toes being reflected under them, so that there may be seal fur on one toe and red on its neighbour and this is reflected in the black and pink of the pads under the two toes concerned.

It is simple enough to understand these two series—the tabby-points and the tortie-points. People will have their own views on the cats; some will greatly admire them, others may criticize; but there is no difficulty in appreciating that tabby-points and tortie-points with seal, blue, chocolate and lilac were able to be bred, have been bred, and fall easily into two categories, with the different colours clearly distinguishable the one from the others. It is not quite so easy to unravel the complexities of the tabby-tortoiseshells.

### TABBY-TORTOISESHELLS

In the points of a tabby-tortoiseshell, the non-yellow patches are the agouti wild-type, with banded hairs, and the stripes or blotches found in tabby cats. The schedule of the 1968 conference described them as Siamese cats showing tabby-tortie pattern on the points.

Such an outburst of colours and patterns must always be a joy to anyone inclined towards experimental breeding. It is possible to breed a litter comprising kittens with many different points: self-coloured, tabby of one colour or another, and various tortoiseshell females. The probablities from a given mating can be worked out; and in view of the fact that Siamese kittens are born white, with the points colour beginning to show in about a week (see Chapter 5) it is easy to imagine the eagerness with which the breeder watches for the appearance of colour in the points of his very young kittens.

Chapter four

# Pets and neuters

Siamese cats are at their very best as pets because they are, as a breed, insistent upon human companionship. All varieties of *felis domesticus* seek out man and share his habitat, and most cats show him affection; but Siamese are by far the most forthcoming, giving their devotion to their human owners, showing sorrow if their people are away and joy when they return, shouting their delight and running to and fro with excitement and pleasure at being re-united with the loved ones. A Siamese will roam about as all cats do if he be free, but he will come back often, seeking out the society of his people and showing quite clearly that, greedy little pig though he is, it is not only for food that he comes purring, and giving little licks and love-bites to the hand of his chosen human.

It is perfectly possible for a breeding queen to be a pet cat as well as a mother; Salween Fairmaid, long since gone to the happy hunting grounds, was my constant companion as well as being the dam of some very fine kittens; but in general, the feelings of a breeding queen are principally concerned with the reproduction cycle, so that affectionate towards humans though she may be, they are not her main preoccupation. Stud cats might well be pets, but (as fully discussed in Chapter 6) it is impossible to have them in the house, and therefore they cannot be companions to their owners; a full male is an agreeable creature, more often than not, but no one can put up with a house that 'smells of tom-cat', so stud cats must always have their own separate quarters. For those who want the companionship of these cats, it is much best to have a neuter.

### NEUTERING

Neutering a male is a slight operation; it is for his vet.-surgeon to say at what age he wishes a kitten to be neutered—it will be three or four months; there is a law against neutering a male kitten over six months old under a local anaesthetic, and therefore it is best to have this small piece of surgery carried out when the kitten is young; although a cat can be neutered at any age and indeed, a male neutered after he is adult and has, perhaps, sired a litter or so of kittens, is likelier than a jejune kitten to keep the slender lines of his body. To spay a female is a longer operation which, obviously, can only be performed under a general anaesthetic; but it is not regarded by experienced vet.-surgeons as being a difficult or a dangerous thing; the technique of spaying a female kitten has been brought to perfection since this operation became known in the Fancy, about forty years ago; it is not even a very expensive undertaking. Once again, it is for the vet.-surgeon to say at what age it shall.be carried out.

### KEEPING A PET

There are differences of opinion as to whether a male or a female Siamese will make the better pet; it has been said that the males are always fonder of their human friends than are the 'utterly selfish girls'; this probably referred to a queen who was not spayed. People who buy Siamese kittens as pets are often quite definite in their requirements: the kitten for them must be a boy, or must be a girl. It is or ought to be a pleasure to deal with those who know their own minds: a breeder who has only females left and is asked for a male can usually supply names and addresses of friends in the fancy who may be able to help. In fact, quite a high percentage of owners of pet cats prefer the females.

One of the joys of owning a Siamese is that there are no two alike; those who have had pet Siamese of both sexes would be hard put to it to say which they preferred, while admitting that the ways and behaviour of the cats were not by any means identical. It is sometimes supposed that to neuter a cat will spoil its appearance, but this is not necessarily the case. There are classes for both male and female neuters at all the big shows, where they may compete for challenge certificates towards premiership—the equivalent, for a neuter, of a championship—and for premier of premier status, as well as for best-neuter-in-show awards. Some of the cats which appear in the Siamese neuter classes are extremely beautiful, many having retained the svelte lines of a really good show cat in spite of having been neutered.

A well-loved neuter leads a very happy life, though the increase in the number of cars on the roads has somewhat curtailed a cat's liberty. In earlier times, hardly more than twenty years ago, it was reasonable for a neutered cat, even if he were an expensive Siamese, to have his freedom to come and go at will; this liberty was, in fact, extended to breeding queens as recently as the 1950s, when a well-known breeder announced disconsolately, 'I don't know what to do, nor when they will start calling; I keep on letting them out, and then snatching them in again. . . .' There was, thus, a constant worry for the breeder for fear of a mis-mating; but in those so-recent days, it had not yet occurred to owners to enclose their cats unless for some definite reason, such as illness, or kittening. Stud cats were shut in their own premises, but most queens and practically all neuters ran the risk of battles, of infection from strays—and of getting themselves lost.

The anguish of losing a loved animal defies description. His master believes he is in the house or garden, hiding: he will turn up at the next mealtime; perhaps he is in an outhouse—surely he will come when he is hungry. Distracted by this time, the owner runs about, opening the same doors, calling, calling, running into the road to look. The police and the RSPCA or the Humane Association are alerted, the neighbours are told, the miserable owner goes in wider and wider circles round the neighbourhood, calling. . . . Night comes and daylight comes, and the landscape is hopelessly empty—and then, more often than not, milord walks in, and the willing slave, however much he has suffered, imagining his lovely cat trapped, hurt, unable to get home, will welcome him, almost sobbing with relief, while preparing choice viands for the hungry little sinner, who will show great delight at being home, and will probably expect everyone to be pleased to see him! It is a mistake to give up hope at once; there is a true story, recently told, of a poor blind Siamese who strayed, maybe following a dog, and was lost. His owners advertised their loss far and wide, and finally bought a new kitten; but after a month someone from four miles away rang them up to say 'we have your cat'. Hardly believing it, they went along and found him—emaciated and covered with sheep-ticks. This tale has a peculiarly happy ending, for the new kitten and the blind cat took an instant liking for each other, and have become firm friends. The search for a missing Siamese is easier than for another cat by reason of his deep voice; if you shout his name and listen as you go along he will, if you pass close enough to him, answer, and you will hear him.

This same deep voice is a delight to those who like it, and an irritation to those who do not; Siamese are inclined to talk—sometimes to ask for food or to be let in or out, often just for conversation. For those who like cats but do not like their baritone voice, so different from any other cat's that it cannot be described as a 'mew', it is better to have a pet from another breed! But for those who like it, it is a great help when they want to know where their cat is: call his name and he will, unless he decides to play hide-and-seek, answer loud and clear.

## GENERAL CARE

The researches and discoveries of mankind in the fields of medicine and hygiene have greatly aided *felis domesticus* in the struggle for survival; but the internal combustion engine has produced a new danger, and a great many cats no longer likely to contract feline infectious enteritis are killed every year on our roads. This may in some way be a redressing of the balance, but it is a headache for owners of well-loved cats. A blue-pointed cat of mine, Belhaven Columbine, who lived to be 16½, which is a good age for a Siamese, would never go outside her own grounds; but many Siamese do go out, and their owners have to reckon with the probability of a fatal encounter; indeed, for a cat known to cross a busy road, it is not a probability: it is, sooner or later, a certainty. Few can be like the astonishing little factory cat who sat staring at the traffic lights until they were green and then crossed with dignified aplomb! Most people living near traffic have to enclose their cat unless they are so fortunate as to have one who is afraid of the road, or to live right off the beaten track. There are many ways of arranging safety measures; some people even go so far as to have the entire garden netted so that their pet cannot get out; this would have to be a small garden and, even so, it must mean a lot of trouble. A breeder, of course, must have ground space devoted to his cats, and it must include outdoor 'runs'; but plenty of people who own neutered Siamese arrange for their pets to have outdoor enclosures—as it were, gardens of their own. These ought to have a tree or a stropping-post, and a shelter against inclement weather; if possible there should be growing things: small bushes, or even weeds or wildflowers, for a cat loves a 'hidey-hole'. Some of these gardens are arranged so that they lead from a cat-house which in turn leads into the owner's kitchen or lobby; thus by a series of slats, he can ensure the safety of the cat. The enclosure should be sizable so that, as a well-known breeder said recently, 'They really *can run*'.

Pet Siamese in big towns are sometimes to be seen walking out on leads with their owners; it seems a trifle unnatural but it is better than no fresh air at all, though most towns are rapidly becoming unfit for pets except those whose owners live on the outskirts. City cats who enjoy roof-gardens are, incidentally, not unknown. It does not do to be overanxious about a pet. The Victorians used to talk quite crossly about loving parents who spoiled their children, or affectionate owners who overfed their pet animals. You might hear a stern Victorian nannie say of a fat pug or an overpetted child, 'They are killing him with kindness'. Rather severe, perhaps, nevertheless we must take care not to kill our Siamese cats with kindness. Never was a breed more loved, almost adored, than the Siamese; and their owners sometimes err through a sort of exaggerated anxiety. Every breeder knows, for instance, that the cats require to be groomed; in the wild, where nature sees to everything, the loose fur in a cat's coat is pulled out by brambles as he makes his way through undergrowth. In domestication, the cat will try to comb his moulting fur away with his rough little tongue, and maybe swallow or aspirate the 'combings', and do himself harm. So it is best to take a small steel comb to his coat every morning, and this he greatly appreciates: Siamese will queue up at grooming time, seeming to say, as one breeder put it, 'Ooh . . . ! She's going to do me next.'

But some people do not stop at grooming the coats. Some say, 'You ought to clean your cats' ears out every day with cotton wool soaked in a suitable spirit.' In fact, the insides of cats' ears are nearly always perfectly clean. The ear is a delicate member; if a cat scratches his ears or shakes them in discomfort, it is vitally important to get veterinary advice at once, and to carry out the doctor's instructions with precision, for there are many conditions which can affect a feline ear. But if there is nothing wrong, then a policy of non-interference is much the best; to 'mess about' with a healthy animal may start trouble. It is never wise to *look* for worries: so long as a cat is ticking over nicely, it is a mistake for the owner to set up a self-torture department for the purpose of stuffing him full of unneeded medicines or sticking a match stick wrapped in cotton wool into a perfectly healthy ear. No need, however much we love them, to 'kill our Siamese with kindness'.

It may be heresy to say so, but it does not do to assume that because someone has owned Siamese for a long time, he will necessarily be right in everything he advises. Experienced breeders are the best people from whom to seek advice; but you can always check by applying the commonsense test! When I first owned Siamese, a very well-known breeder told me never to use sawdust in scratchingtrays: the cats would get it into their fur, aspirate it, and choke. This was so obviously good, sound sense that only a fool would have disregarded it. But when an eager little beaver gratuitously told me that I must never let the cats go out in bad weather because 'Siamese are so delicate, they might catch cold,' well—that did not make sense and it still does not! Siamese are no more delicate than any other cat, and those that go out in all weathers are more likely to withstand any germs they may meet than those who are kept in a hot-house atmosphere. What is important is that there should be shelter and warmth available for them when they want it.

## FEEDING

Feeding, also, is a matter of commonsense. If a Siamese be overfed, he will become fat, and his appearance will be spoilt; but never, never be misled into underfeeding him; let no one tell you that his elegant slinkiness can best be preserved by 'giving only small meals'. Any healthy cat should have a healthy appetite; no animal can grow to strong adulthood, mother healthy young or sire the right kind of progeny without adequate sustenance. A growing kitten, a brood queen, a stud cat—they all ought to have grand appetites. To find the happy medium only needs commonsense: choice morsels between meals are a poor idea, huge meals for neuters are absurd; but three good meals a day are not too many for kittens or studs, and a queen in kitten or rearing kittens can eat all day without spoiling her looks.

Siamese can eat with advantage almost any fresh food—beef, ox heart, all fresh fish, and game. The cats have individual tastes: some would rather drink water than milk; many will joyfully accept fresh cooked rabbit while refusing to touch frozen rabbit. Liver now and then is a good thing, though given too often it may be 'loosening'; raw beef is essential—the best food that could possibly be given. Sardines once a week are not a bad idea—much easier than possibly having to administer a small dose of liquid paraffin. Endless cat foods are marketed in tins and packets, and these are perfectly wholesome, but they ought only to be used to supplement a diet of fresh food. Some of the foods sold in biscuit form are much appreciated, and are useful to give to a cat who complains, perhaps late at night, that he is hungry again and expects something to be done about it! Growing grass ought to be available for the cats if possible; Siamese living in the country will often kill mice, voles and the like, and may even sometimes give themselves a 'tummy-upset' by devouring their prey. Birds, alas, are 'fair game' to the cats—but they are, fortunately, often difficult for them to catch.

### BEHAVIOUR

In the matter of behaviour, it has to be remembered that there are no two cats exactly alike, just as there are no two people exactly alike (excepting, of course, uni-ovular twins). The results of this inequality are many and varied. If all our cats were alike to look at, there would be no cat shows; if they all had equal resistance to illness, there would be far fewer problems for their vet.-surgeons; if they all had the same degree of roadsense, then either they would caper joyously wherever the fancy took them and we should have to keep them all enclosed; or they would be like Nedda, who never put a paw outside her own gate, and then they could all go free most of the time, which would be splendid. In fact, their inequalities are part of their charm. There is the delightful Siamese who will purr for anyone; the playful one, who keeps his kitten ways into adulthood; the greedy cat, the bold little thief, the cuddly cat, the scornful one from whom a rare caress is such a joy. Some Siamese are timid, and their need for protection is very appealing to the one person they trust. Some are extremely intelligent: I have seen in one litter a sharp-witted little scoundrel, always on the ball, and a pleasant, dreamy, slow kitten, obviously the fool of the family!

No two alike, yet all charming. Which is more than can always be said for our own race. There is an owner who hit her cat because he came second in his Open Class at a show. It seems incredible that anyone could be so cruel and so stupid. Presumably she is so foolish that, hoping for top honours and being disappointed she lost her temper and lashed out at a creature who could not possibly know why he had been struck. Clever or not, conforming to the standards or not, these creatures are innocent: they have thrown in their lot with man, they are utterly dependent on us. It is dreadful to think that they may be shut up in small cages; ill-nourished; used only as money-spinners; or left to the mercy of unimaginative fools. It does happen that man's idiocy inflicts cruelty on these exquisite creatures whose destiny it is to be quite dependent upon us. Though no two are alike, they have this in common: they need our kindness.

Differences of temperament can be important to pet-owners; more than one Siamese cat goes where his humans go, is absolutely at ease in any hotel, even to the extent of sharing the fire with a dog if one happens to be there, and remains calm no matter what circumstances may arise. This is, of course, partly usage: people who get a Siamese as a kitten and treat him as a member of the family can expect that he will be trusting; but the cat with the naturally placid temperament is the one most likely to feel no fear of strangers or of strange surroundings.

These cats always get on well with their own dog—the one whose home they share; however terrified a cat or kitten may be the first time he is in close proximity with a dog, the two will be sharing the hearth in due course.

Those who love Siamese do so not only for their unusual and striking appearance but because their behaviour towards mankind is not quite the same as that of other breeds. They have a fondness for us; we ought not, however, to imagine that they think as we do. Man is the only animal capable of conceptual thought. Nevertheless there are ideas in the head of a Siamese cat; he cannot formulate a chain of reasoning, yet his actions are not always purely instinctive. The simplest urge of the cat is to get food—whether he is hungry or not. Suppose there is milk available and he is a cat who likes it (some, of course, prefer water) then he will drink it—instinctively. But suppose the milk is in a bottle, sealed as left by the supplier? I have seen a Siamese go round the top, edging it off with her lower teeth; and when the top was quite free, up came her paw, over went the bottle, and the formica table-cover was a sea of milk—for her to lap. It was a variant of the well-known performance of dipping a paw into the narrow-necked milk-jug and licking the milk off an elegant Siamese glove; and it was a most calculated and slick affair! Surely, some sort of thought-process here?

However the proof that there are ideas and even thoughts in the masked heads of these felines lies in the fact that not only in appearance, not only in tastes or character, but in intelligence also there are no two exactly alike. And the moment you admit to degrees of intelligence, you admit to there being intelligence to start with: to have more or less of any quality you must have that quality present. People who love Siamese cats can only judge of their psychological ideas by their actions. The cat who is always rubbing against us, purring, following us everywhere, is the one whose mind is full of love; the one who goes forth alone, comes home when he will, orders his own life, is the independent, self-sufficient cat; the little wretch who is always in trouble, knocking things over, stealing food, running away—and expecting to be welcomed no matter what crimes he has committed—is the mischievous boy of the party. Of course, to steal food or to expect affection may well be instinctive reactions; but if you watch your Siamese friend, you will discover behaviour which certainly suggests that something like thought goes on in his mind. Nedda, the blue-point who knew that roads are dangerous, had a friend in the next property, a red neuter known as Sandy who also understood the dangers of the road. Together they roamed the gardens and fields and woods, met in a grass-grown lane at dusk, and caught shrew-mice. But whereas Nedda spent many a rainy afternoon in a convenient out-house in Sandy's garden, he was never allowed in her garden, but driven out if he ever ventured to enter it; he was her friend, but he had to be kept away from her humans and from any kittens that there might be; she would meet Sandy on neutral ground or on his premises, but he was not welcome at her home. Then came the freezing winter of 1962, and in Sandy's home there was trouble with the watermains, so that Sandy's master came to us to fill large cans from our taps and, in the springtime, dangerous men came into Sandy's garden and pulled up a lot of it, and remade the mains with frightful hammerings, rendering the place unfit for any cat to be happy in. Nedda went into the lane, and called through the hedge, and said 'Ee-oo!' Which, being interpreted, meant: 'Your garden isn't any use, so you can come into mine, if you like.'

I know this is a correct interpretation, for through the hedge came Sandy, and sat on the brick terrace beside the aubretia, and his Siamese friend graciously welcomed him. So that there was certainly a thought, or an idea of some sort, in her head. Siamese cats are worth studying, for their minds are full of interest for those who love them. We should not like it if our animals were suddenly to resemble us in thinking as we do; a cat who could remember the past, foresee coming events, feel pity, develop a speech centre, and perhaps be sardonic, would not be a cat at all, and would be most undesirable! However, these cats are capable of ideas.

## BOARDING CATTERIES

One of the difficulties encountered by Siamese owners is that of having to decide what shall be done with their pet while they are away for a holiday. If the house is to be shut up, the cat must go to a boarding cattery, or to a friend. Sometimes it is possible to arrange with a neighbour to come in and feed him, and to leave an egress for him to go in and out; it is a moot point whether it is best to leave him quite alone but on his accustomed home ground or to send him away to a strange place where someone responsible will look after him but where he will be enclosed in a small space in new surroundings. If it is decided to send him away, it is of the utmost importance for the owner to inspect the place where he is going. There are plenty of boarding catteries, some run on a professional basis, some by private individuals; inevitably, some are very good, and other not quite so good. If the cat's owner has not had a recommendation from someone he can trust, he ought to go and inspect the premises for himself. He should understand that the important point is not 'Will my cat be unhappy?' but 'Will he remain in good health?' In such catteries it is usual for the boarders to be put in separate small houses, each with a short run, suitably wire-netted. No one can guarantee that one of the cats will not fall ill; the responsibility for the person in charge is heavy; a visitor may come looking well and develop a high temperature during the night. The really good proprietor of a boarding cattery is the one who can see trouble quickly: even, maybe, see that a visitor is not himself and refuse him entry; in any case, discover at once if anything looks like being wrong, and whip the cat concerned into isolation. All such catteries should have a small 'chalet' away from the rows of 'houses and gardens', into which a suspect can instantly be put. The place where a cat's health is safe is the one where the proprietors take care of the visitors themselves and are keen-eyed to see any possible trouble. A kind, gentle person who puts large plates of food down for the boarders and strokes and pets them is not necessarily the best person to look after them.

Anyone inspecting a cattery with a view to sending in his cat while he is on holiday should look to see how neat and clean the pens are; whether there are plates of food left untouched; if there are, then either the cat is not hungry or the food is unpalatable. Charges are high, and with reason, for the work involved in running a boarding cattery and the expense of upkeep, heating and feeding are all considerable. The person paying, however, puts his cat's life in the cattery proprietor's hands; petting and 'homey' surroundings are as nothing when compared with health, for without health, nothing can be enjoyed.

It would be easy to give a list of excellent boarding catteries for Siamese cats, just as it would be easy to give the names and addresses of club secretaries; but it would be of no use. A club may appoint at any moment for a variety of reasons a different secretary with a different address; and the splendid boarding cattery of today may change hands tomorrow, and be less well-run—or may even close down. In Britain the best way for a complete novice to obtain news concerning the cats is for him to buy a copy of *Fur and Feather*. This is, as its title implies, a journal devoted to the interests of birds and small furred animals. It is the official organ of the Governing Council of the Cat Fancy, and appears fortnightly; under *Cats and Catdom* it prints reports of cat shows, articles by well-known breeders, letters from club secretaries concerning club activities, and Governing Council notices including lists of shows. This is a journal which concerns all cats, and therefore those desiring information on Siamese only may not find exactly what they want in the first issue they buy; but there are frequent notices from the various Siamese societies and there are also advertisements of cats at stud and kittens for sale. As discussed in Chapter 9, other countries also have their periodicals, such as the important and comprehensive magazine *Cats* in the USA.

### BUYING KITTENS

Siamese kittens are advertised for sale in many papers—the big dailies, the 'local' Press, and various periodicals; it is well to remember that merchandise is not necessarily good because it is advertised in a reputable journal. People who are complete novices, folk who have 'fallen for' Siamese cats are usually eager to buy a kitten at once; but it is better to look around a bit first, and at all costs to see the kitten in his own surroundings. If the kitten is required for show, or to breed from, it is vitally important to learn something about the breed by going to shows, seeing the best and becoming acquainted with fanciers. Unfortunately there are people who breed kittens of indifferent show quality and sell them for low prices on the 'small profits, quick returns' principle. It is necessary to beware of such folk. A proper price for a really fine show specimen is £60, and for a pet £25—but for that price one should expect the best; in America, you can pay anything up to $400. For a kitten who is to be a neutered pet an amount varying from £60–£80 may be asked; the most important thing for the purchaser in a pet as in a show kitten is the matter of health. Is the new kitten kept in good conditions, are his brothers and sisters healthy, have there been deaths in his dam's litters? Health is far more important than wealth, for without it nothing at all can be a pleasure; it is even more important than love: to find yourself with a sickly pet is heartbreaking, and anyone wanting a Siamese kitten for the first time should tell himself that it is worth while to be patient and to make a few enquiries.

It is, however, not true that Siamese are 'delicate'; they are as tough as any alley cat if they are properly bred and cared for; inbreeding would wreck any breed, as would bad living conditions, but breeders are aware of this and a good deal of outcrossing has been done—notably in the red-points and tabby-points—so that it is perfectly possible to obtain a strong pet cat who is also good-looking. He or she will have to be neutered and will prove to be very affectionate and a charming companion with, as all healthy young creatures should have, a hearty appetite. Obviously, meat has to be cut very finely for tiny kittens, and chopped into less small pieces as they grow. Sometimes a Siamese will refuse anything frozen; this is probably because the process of freezing takes away from the scent of the food.

These cats are practically always house-trained. The moment a tiny kitten starts to eat for himself he will use a scratch-tray. A scratch-tray should always be provided at first—with earth, peat, perhaps paper—even if the kitten is to have the freedom of the garden as he grows. If any 'mistakes' should occur, which is not very likely, the kitten will understand if you growl at him—which is what his dam would have done in similar circumstances.

### INTELLIGENCE

Siamese are, as a breed, clever. While accepting that the cat is not capable of conceptual thought; while realising that the owner who talks to his cat as to another human, trying to put human thought-processes into the animal's mind, and assuring his friends that his pet understands every word said, is plainly ridiculous; yet science has it that the cortex of the cat is sufficiently developed for him to be capable of receiving ideas and acting on them. This is certainly true. The mother who folds a blanket neatly across her kittens before going out is doing more than just the scrabbling which stems from the instinctive wish to hide the precious secret from predators: she is not incapable of a chain of reasoning, albeit a short chain. Many of the cat's actions are instinctive: he smells fish, goes towards it and asks for it, for instance. But some cats will do some things that others will not do: some Siamese will watch birds go across the television screen, turning their heads to follow the birds' flight; others are not interested. Some will fetch a woollen ball and set it at their owner's feet, and pat his leg to induce him to throw the ball, which they will retrieve as often as it is thrown for them; others will never learn to play this game. Some Siamese will pick up a kitten, not necessarily their own, and put it into shelter on a wet day; others would never think of such a thing. The cats have no speech centre; they do not think of yesterday nor of tomorrow; but they have thought-processes of a kind, and these are sufficient for their needs.

A great deal has been said about extra-sensory perception in the cat, and nothing much has been proved; to be sure of such reactions and their causes, you need tests carried out in laboratory conditions. I know that one of my Siamese queens goes to the door minutes before the butcher arrives—long before I can hear his van. He comes at any time between 3 and 4 o'clock, and she knows, well before I could, that he is on the way. Perhaps her sense of hearing is extra sharp; what she does in this respect proves nothing—but it suggests a line of enquiry.

Cats have been associated in men's minds with witchcraft; and a

Siamese, with his long legs, his vivid blue eyes in a dark mask and his startling appearance when in fighting trim, may well seem unearthly! But he is a cat, with all a cat's attributes, even though in him, with his unusual love of mankind, these attributes may be rather exaggerated. Certainly some have quicker reactions than have others. I can remember the fool of the family—a family of four months old—sitting gazing into space, looking like a picture post-card kitten, while a weasel came under the netting of the cat's enclosure, and stared at him. Long before I could recover from the paralysis which beset me, his much smaller brother reacted like mercury in a storm: the weasel never made a sound—the kitten took him in the throat, and bit to kill. He dropped his prey, picked it up amidships, and came down the enclosure with even the big cats standing back respectfully while he started a triumphal banquet in which they were, presently, allowed to join. Another quick reaction becomes evident if at meal time you drop an extra tit-bit onto a dish: some cats ignore the morsel, others snap it up almost before it reaches the plate. Their mothers will usually teach kittens to catch mice. You can see them very quiet in a circle in the long grass, waiting, until suddenly the dam shoots out a long arm and starts the mouse, and one of the kittens gets it. Thus they are handed over to their new owners already accomplished mousers.

A pet cat is the better for grooming (fully discussed in Chapter 5) just as is a show cat; and to rub his coat over, after combing, with a chamois leather, will produce a wonderful sheen—as well as a great deal of purring. Extra attention means extra time and trouble—but it will be repaid by a great deal of affection and a wonderful companionship. Such a cat will follow his particular human everywhere; always want to be with him; give him all his devotion. Indeed, with his fidelity, his intelligence and his beauty, there is no pet quite like a Siamese.

Chapter five

# Care and health

In the last decade of the nineteenth century and the first years of the twentieth, knowledge of feline ailments was practically nil. During the last fifty years, veterinary science has increased with great speed as, of course, has medicine in general: war is always the mother of inventiveness, and the two great wars of the present century have spurred the minds of men to great and fruitful efforts in all branches of knowledge, technological, biological, astronomical —an endless chain of new awareness, in which the links join, as chemistry and physics have done, and on which are strung the dark stones of destruction and the bright jewels of happiness.

Research into feline ailments has been a joyful thing for those who brought the Siamese cat to the West. Probably the first effective vaccine against feline infectious enteritis was produced in a research laboratory in the USA; I can remember, nearly thirty years ago, that one of my Siamese queens had a new litter and a friend said 'I can get you some American Vaccine'. I think that this was the Lederer vaccine, and it may be that America shares with Switzerland the honour of being first to protect cats from this killer disease.

The advances in veterinary science of the last 20 years have, naturally, benefited cats including Siamese as well as other animals. There are all over the world research centres where animal diseases are studied and many of these centres have departments for research into feline ailments; new drugs and new methods of treatment are constantly appearing. A great deal has been said and written on the subject of health in Siamese cats, and much that was useful even a decade ago is now out-of-date. The basic requirements, however, remain constant. In particular, if a cat seems to be ill, send for your veterinary adviser; delay can be disastrous. Never, if you are satisfied there is something really wrong, let yourself be guided by a layman, nor by literature produced by an unqualified person. Owners should attend at all times to the matter of hygiene; floors, walls, baskets, blankets ought to be clean—not just surface-clean, but scrubbed and rubbed clean. As mentioned in Chapter 3, all cats require to be groomed once a day; they ought to be brushed, combed, or finger-groomed. One of our judges told me years ago 'I prefer hand-grooming'; undoubtedly in this way nothing can be missed that could be wrong with a cat's coat; should there be a scratch or a bit of skin trouble, the owner's fingers would find it.

The advice to keep a cat's quarters very clean and to give him daily grooming is not unreasonable. The domestic cat has thrown in his lot with us and we have accepted him: he is no longer a wild animal, and we have to see to it that he goes along with us as our civilisation develops. Strange as it may seem to us, 200 years ago it was quite usual for a gentleman in a satin coat to take a bath very seldom and to harbour small parasites; today, breeders of repute will not tolerate cat-fleas in the coats of Siamese kittens—and this is right.

### KITTEN FLEAS

The cat is the cleanest of creatures, and an adult cat goes a long way to attend to his own toilet. But in warm weather these parasites, peculiar to cats and not using any other animal as host, will appear in the fur of kittens, and their dam may need help to eradicate them. It is a good idea to keep a container of special dusting-powder, made for cats and sold by good pet shops, and by chemists, and to rub a little into the coats of kittens each day from the time of their birth. In this way, they will probably never have any fleas at all; but it is important to use only properly recommended powder so that it will be safe for the queen to swallow, for she will certainly wash her kittens. Veterinary instruction is that these cat-fleas do not lay their eggs only in the cats' fur, but in crevices in floors and so on, so that there is always risk of re-infection; thus, scrubbed floors and daily grooming are really important.

### ROUNDWORM (ASCARIS)

Another very tiresome parasite which cats harbour is the roundworm and this, also, manages to leave eggs in corners of even the cleanest premises. It is the advice of veterinary surgeons that anyone who breeds or shows cats, or keeps a good number, should treat them for roundworm at regular intervals. A suggested course of treatment is two doses of Coopane with an interval of eight days every three months. Each and every feline on the premises should be so treated whether any sign of worms has been observed or not. It would be a complete waste of time if you had, say, four cats living together and only one had shown signs of worms to dose just that one cat: if he or she had not passed on this unpleasant parasite to at least one of the others, this would be nothing less than miraculous. So, to clear the worms from one while another was incubating more, would simply leave a vicious circle. Kittens must not be given such big doses as adult cats; in the case of Coopane, half a tablet can be administered to a big kitten or a quarter to a small kitten. This is quite easily given by hand; the tiny ones in particular will allow their mouths to be opened and their quarter-tablets to be slipped down their throats, and will swallow them without giving any trouble. Older cats, however, are more wily, and it is therefore fortunate that Coopane is practically tasteless: crush a tablet on a chopping-board with the rolling-pin, cut up the cat's favourite food (raw liver, if he likes it, absorbs the powder well) on top of the powder thus obtained, wiping the rolling-pin with a piece of the meat so that he gets the full dose—and he will probably eat it all up and lick the board. This is not invariably the case; there can be individuals who, somehow, detect a foreign flavour, so that sterner measures have to be taken. But I have only, in many years of breeding, owned one Siamese who would not take Coopane in food. If you crush a tablet and put a touch of the resultant powder on the tip of your own tongue, it has a very faintly salty taste, no more. This treatment is valuable and it has the advantage of being able to be used with perfect safety for a queen in kitten.

It seems almost incredible that in properly kept premises these parasites could gain a footing, leaving eggs which are not removed by the disinfection and constant cleansing of catteries; yet vet.-surgeons say that it happens. In addition, a cat may go to a show, or to kennels while his owners are away; a queen may visit a stud, and a male will receive many visiting queens. All these are possible sources of infection by that nasty little pest the roundworm; there is every reason for dosing the cats regularly. Indeed, a kitten badly infested will have constant diarrhoea and may eventually die: 'Worms will not do serious harm to an adult but they can kill a kitten.'[1] It must be remembered that kittens are growing; deprived of food by the worms, the poor little host will starve. It is usual for round-worm to be brought up from the stomach, but this does not always happen, and it is as well to remember the possibility of these parasites, which do not invariably make their presence known and so may be missed.

### CARE OF THE EYES

It is necessary to remember that the eyes of a Siamese kitten will open soon after birth; they are very often already half-open when the kitten is born. The kittens must not be left in a strong light, or they will develop 'sticky' eyes. It is as well to have a thin curtain across the window for the first week or ten days of their lives.

Penicillin has been and is of enormous value to the cats. Should a cat be severely bitten either in a fight with a neighbouring cat or by some other animal, it is important that he should receive early treatment with penicillin; results are wonderful, but if there be delay, sepsis may occur.

### RINGWORM

There is a new treatment for ringworm: a drug called griseofulvin, given in tablet form by mouth. Veterinary advice is that a cat with ringworm, so easily discovered under the short, largely pale coat of a regularly-groomed Siamese, should be put in isolation because the condition is highly infectious to other animals and to man. It is quite easy to isolate a cat, even a Siamese, except from the person who looks after him and administers his tablets; Ringworm is an illness which clears up quickly, both in cats and in man, if it be suitably treated. Indeed, there is no better advice than this for any owner of Siamese cats: if something seems wrong for more than half-a-day, consult your veterinary surgeon. If there is nothing serious, no harm has been done; if there is, the cat's life may be saved.

### VACCINATION

Inoculation against feline infectious enteritis is enormously important. This condition is scientifically termed panleucopenia, and research laboratories have worked for many years now to produce vaccines that would be a protection against it. Vaccines at present used are made from an attenuated strain of the virus concerned, and produce a very high antibody response. It will be understood that a vaccine does not kill anything: it consists of a-virulent disease germs which stimulate the blood of the individual inoculated to produce the antibodies which are its defence against the illness in question. These antibodies are nature's army, always present to combat any invading force of disease germs; but such an invasion may be too strong for the defences: inoculation with a dead or a-virulent vaccine stimulates the organism concerned to produce extra antibodies, and these reinforcements will be present to deal summarily with any attackers. One advantage of a modern vaccine is the high antibody level which it produces, and another is that since the virus is not shed following inoculation, immunity is long-lasting. It is administered subcutaneously at ten weeks, and it will produce immunity within seventy-two hours; as with all previous vaccines it must never be given to a cat already sick, nor to a queen in kitten. However, it is recommended that a 'booster shot' should be administered after two years. Inoculation is not cheap—up to £5 per kitten; but anyone who has seen a cat with this illness, dehydrated, wretched, in pain and with staring coat, will agree that no price could be too high for the protection which it gives. Your vet.-surgeon will know which vaccine to use, and at what age.

### ONYXECTOMY

One modern discovery concerns onyxectomy. Science has found out how to draw the claws of cats without danger to their health. Everyone knows that a cat may be very bad for valuable furniture, it is his nature to keep his claws in trim by stropping them on the bark of a tree. Most people have seen cats standing on their tip-toes furiously stropping the claws of their front paws on a tree: this is a part of their toilet. Living as they do in our houses, cats will use our furniture for their 'manicure'; the legs of old-fashioned kitchen tables, made of plain unvarnished wood are much favoured for this purpose; shiny, polished wood is not of use to them, but they may claw stair-carpets, leather and any silken, woollen or cotton material. If you instal a stropping-post for a cat who has no access to a garden with trees in it, this will protect your furnishings; such posts, some of them most artistically carved in the semblance of trees, are manufactured by makers of feline accessories, and Siamese cat owners have found them of help. Sometimes there will be a cat who cannot learn not to touch furniture, but Siamese are, as a breed, so intelligent that many can be taught that it is wrong rapturously to tear a few threads from the sofa—or at least may understand that it is displeasing to their owner; always given that the owner remembers the oft-repeated advice: if you want your cat to know you are displeased, do not shout at him nor hit him; he simply will not understand. Growl at him and he will realise that you are displeased. As his dam growled at him when he was tiny if he mistook the cat-house floor for the scratch-tray, teaching him to be clean, so you may teach him not to touch the furnishings. There was once a television programme in which viewers were told that two Siamese cats left all night in a room with an armchair in it would destroy the chair utterly; the impression was given that Siamese more than any other breed would destroy it. In fact, the intelligence of a Siamese may well enable him to learn not to touch furnishings. Not everyone, of course, has the patience to teach him this lesson.

There is a factor which has always been present in human history: fashion. Years ago, rich people would buy a Siamese cat in order to own an exotic pet; often the happiness of the cat depended upon the possibility of there being a cat-lover among the domestic staff—and there frequently was such a person. The owner wanted the cat only so that he could boast of possessing a rare creature. Today it is said that the Siamese cat is a status symbol: it is not quite so bad to be without a Siamese cat as to be without a washing-machine, but we have a situation in which many are owned by people who feed and house them well but, having bought them for fashion's sake, do not truly love them. Among such people are quite a few who are not unnaturally attached to the furnishings of their homes and are confronted with the stropping problem. It has been found that a cat can be declawed quite painlessly, and it is no wonder that people who own a Siamese for the sake of prestige and who find their new three-piece suite being torn by the cat will have an onyxectomy performed on him if they hear that it can be done safely. This operation is, in fact, advocated by some qualified persons, and it is not surprising to find laymen accepting what is told to them by a qualified adviser.

No cat which has been declawed can be shown at any show run

under the rules of the Governing Council of the Cat Fancy. Nor may a declawed cat appear in a championship class at a show promoted with the sanction of the Cat Fanciers Association in America; the relevant rule runs 'A cat not having . . . claws . . . may not receive *any* award in a championship class.' Article VI section 7 of the rules of the American Cat Association, revised in 1969, has 'No declawed cats may be shown'. These rules show disapproval of this newly-devised practice. The reason is that a declawed cat is a maimed cat. He cannot repel an attacker, nor climb a tree to escape from an enemy; he is a prey for any creature that may threaten him. He cannot scratch himself; whereas he could use his teeth to cope with an irritating 'tickle' on his body, there is nothing he can do about scratching his neck or his head. After his onyxectomy has been performed he will, sooner or later, jump up onto a chair or shelf; there will be nothing to hold on with and he will slip; no one who has seen the piteous expression of dismay on his face could forget it. Better by far be without a cat than keep one who has deliberately been maimed.

Recent science, though it has produced so much that is good, has also given rise to some mistaken ideas. There have always been cranks in this world, and the brilliant successes of informed psycho-analysis have had their 'fall-out' in the shape of truly dangerous theories applied by persons not really qualified to practise this branch of medicine. Idiotic as it may seem, some practitioners have endeavoured to attribute to psychological factors ill-health in cats. Such persons consider that Siamese are peculiarly prone to psychological disturbances, and one such practitioner asked, with serious interest, whether an emaciated kitten, not doing at all well, was born the first or the last of the litter? This momentous question could not be answered by the breeder, and the kitten was found to have—roundworm; and, consequently, to be starving. We have to beware of cranks; a Siamese cat is well or is ill, but not for psychological reasons. He is not yet so civilised as to hurry and worry himself into illness, and he has no Oedipus complex; his dam loves him just so long as she has milk for him to take; after that, each forgets the other. Of course, if he meets her a year later and she calls to him, he will mate her—and so he would his grand-dam or his great-grand-dam, without recognising them; he is still the natural animal, although he lives in our houses; and any disorders which may attack him have nothing to do with his mental state.

## QUARANTINE LAW

Quarantine law is important for Siamese cats. They are a very popular breed so that there are many of them, and you can find a lot of extremely beautiful Siamese abroad. Plenty of folk come home from distant lands and would like to bring one or more pet Siamese with them and there are people who have purchased cats abroad and brought them to Britain, putting them in approved quarantine catteries for six months before they could take them home. In addition, some breeders would like to take their cats and kittens to shows on the continent and are prevented because quarantine awaits them on their return; for the same reason breeders abroad cannot bring their cats to be exhibited in Britain, for these would have to be placed in kennels immediately on arrival.

Many such people bitterly resent the control exercised by law but the importance of quarantine regulations cannot be overstressed. Except for occasional cases in quarantine kennels there was, until 1969, no rabies in Britain after 1922; our collective memories are short and the people who in that year realised the seriousness of the disease are now old and in the last fifty years many have grown up knowing practically nothing at all about rabies. This is understandable, for until recently there has been nothing to bring the condition to our attention: in the minds of many it must rate with the plague as an anachronism. Those whom it does concern are the farmers, whose cattle can be ruined by the disease but who have largely forgotten a state of affairs not encountered in the British Isles for the greater part of half-a-century; and the pet-owners who wish, or have heard that their friends wish, to bring in a dog or a cat without having to be parted from their pet.

The Animal Health Division of the Ministry of Agriculture, Fisheries and Food, which is the successor to the Veterinary Department of the Privy Council Office first set up in 1865, has often been petitioned by individuals and by corporate bodies to relax, alter or rescind the laws which obtain in respect of importation of animals; and fortunately the Division has always, after careful exploration of all possibilities, refused.

## RABIES

The disease which is known as rabies in animals and as hydrophobia in man leads almost inevitably to madness and death. Whenever it has been written about, stress has been placed upon its canine aspect. This is because the dog is the most dangerous carrier of the condition. It is a disease of the bloodstream, not airborne; its mode of transfer is through a bite or a scratch from a rabid animal, or even a lick on an existing lesion, for it is carried in the saliva of an infected individual. It is possible for a cat with rabies to fly at a man's throat; but the disease often shows itself in the cat as so many feline illnesses do: the affected individual sits sadly, silent, a poor sick cat, refusing food, until the last agony of madness and death comes upon it. Unless the little creature should summon up the energy to lick a wound on the kind hand caressing him, he will probably die without passing the disease to anyone. Because of this he has been less considered and discussed where this matter is concerned than the unfortunate dog, whose symptoms include a desire to wander far afield and to snap at any creature that he meets on his way. The manner in which rabies affects the canine population is dangerous in the extreme. A rabid dog will bite other dogs, cats if he should come across them, cattle and man—in fact, anything which crosses his path.

In the early days of the present century tales were told about Louis Pasteur who, with another biologist called Roux, worked from 1881 on the matter of *rage* and, in 1885 produced a vaccine 'to be used on a man who had received a bite from a rabid dog'. The Pasteur vaccine is a protective vaccine and it was said to be very painful to the patient to whom the treatment is administered; but lately a new and more acceptable form of vaccine has been perfected in France, and there is a charming picture of two cats telling each other that their 'jabs' had been 'comme une caresse'. There is also today a live vaccine—the Flury vaccine—which is used as a preventive for creatures who have not had the disease, but which is by no means a hundred per cent successful; dogs who have been given it and have had 'booster' inoculations have nevertheless contracted the disease and have died.

This illness is, fortunately, not endemic in Britain. There is no reservoir of rabies in any free-living, wild-life animal population in these islands. The condition, if it appears, is brought from abroad. Its results, not least to man, are terrifying: in days of old, euthanasia by suffocation with a pillow was practised, so awful were its effects and so certain its end. It was in 1831 that the government was first stirred to action: it brought in 'A BILL to prevent the spreading of canine madness. . . . Whereas many of His Majesty's Subjects have suffered from the disease occasioned by the bite of Dogs in a rabid state, and in such cases death hath ensued . . . it shall be lawful for any Justice of the Peace or Chief Magistrate, on information or suspicion of the existence of Canine Madness, to issue a public notice, requiring all Dogs within any parish, wapentake, division, city, borough, liberty, township, market town, franchise, hamlet, tithing, precinct and chapelry, mentioned in such notice, to be kept confined during the time therein stated. . . .'[2]

However, in 1889 there were 340 cases of rabies, 312 of them in dogs. The government of the day sought to bring the disease under control by giving powers to local authorities to muzzle dogs, to dispose of strays, and to prohibit the holding of dog shows. These powers having been somewhat loosely exercised, central control was established in 1890 in an act requiring local authorities to enforce their terms, so that no dog might appear in public without a muzzle. It has to be remembered that the dog, one of whose symptoms is the desire to bite, has always been the principal distributor of this disease; a rabid dog free among a flock of sheep can decimate them, and there is a dreadful tale, told in a book published by the Ministry, of the death in 1886 of 257 deer in Richmond Park, where a rabid dog had started the disease. The herd was affected for more than a year—though, as it consisted of controlled domestic animals, the illness was contained and did not spread to other districts.

Once the orders had been strictly enforced by the local authorities, the incidence of the disease decreased. The public complained, however, and criticized, and the orders were rescinded: alas, three years later there were 727 recorded cases of rabies. At last, in 1896, was established central control of importation of animals. One by one, more severe measures were brought in, including registration, muzzling orders, control of imports and quarantine regulations enforced with great efficiency by customs officials; and by 1902 the disease was completely eradicated from the shores of Britain, only to reappear in 1918 when, at the end of the First World War, regulations were relaxed for lack of personnel, and animals were smuggled in as pets by returning soldiers and brought back rabies with them. Since all the nation's energy, manpower and materials had been concentrated on winning the war, veterinary experience was not equal to the task confronting it, and even the question of muzzles was bedevilled by lack of suitable wire.

It will be realised that rabies in animals and hydrophobia in man go hand-in-hand, being but two faces of the same disease. Whether we feel alarmed for ourselves or concerned for our pets, we cannot afford to relax quarantine restrictions; for every time this has been done, the disease has returned. It is no good thinking that all this has little to do with Siamese cats; for there are many of them, and they are just as vulnerable as any other beast. Though emphasis may always be laid upon the dog, the chief spreader of and sufferer from the disease, yet cats can also contract it. There was one case of a cat with rabies in quarantine, in England, early in 1969. In quarantine conditions this could be dealt with: even the other temporary prisoners would suffer no harm, since each is penned quite separately and the condition, though highly contagious, is not airborne. But if this poor cat had been brought into the country free he could quite easily have licked an injured hand or, feeling ill and out-of-sorts, have hit out with extended claws at another cat who approached him or, worse still—because the consequences would be more serious—at a dog, maybe his house-mate.

It is not difficult to imagine the unhappiness of the owner of a pet, quite possibly a Siamese cat, who is parted from his feline friend for a long time; but this is as nothing compared with the cold fear that comes with the realization that a pet animal is affected and must inevitably die a frightful death; let alone the ghastly awareness that the owner has himself contracted the disease. No use at all to say 'cats are comparatively seldom affected; it can't happen here; it won't happen to *my* cat'. It can, and it maybe will, if restrictions are relaxed or rescinded.

In fact, it happened in 1969–70 that three dogs developed this illness after they had been in quarantine for the regulation period. The Minister, together with the Department of Agriculture and Fisheries in Scotland, treated this disastrous event with the seriousness which it required. He set up a Commission of Enquiry, and decreed that animals then in quarantine must remain there until they had completed one year's isolation. In addition, no animals might be brought into the country, except from the Channel Islands, Ireland or the Isle of Man, all rabies-free.

Such decisions will bring disappointment and unhappiness to

quite a few people. They have already brought endless discussion: the incidence of rabies has been for some time increasing in western Europe; a virus can adapt to changing conditions and its character may alter; such matters are true and are talking-points for those interested. The Commission made recommendations which included arrangements for separate runs for animals in quarantine, such as were already built in the excellent Shurlock Row Quarantine Cattery, and in the new, big, quarantine station at Perth in Western Australia. There is no doubt whatever that what has been done and what is being done is right.

## QUARANTINE CATTERIES

It will be a consolation to the owners of cats in quarantine to know that they are not unhappy. There are 45 approved quarantine kennels in Great Britain, and some of these are for cats only. It is heartening to see the arrangements made for them in some of these kennels. They can be visited at any time not only by ministry inspectors but by owners and friends. In the cattery that I have seen, the cats were in firmly-locked, large, separate compartments, each with a shelf to jump onto and a snug little 'cupboard', raised from the ground, in which to sleep or hide; everything was beautifully clean with, to my astonishment, no scent of any sort: not only no unpleasant smell but no 'hospital' smell of disinfectant either. Toys were provided, and trays of grass growing in earth had been put in the pens. The owner of the cattery was not quite happy about this arrangement, which had not worked out exactly as intended! The idea was that the cats would be able to sniff at the fresh, growing grass, and could have a little nibble if they wished; but some, notably a rather larger neuter, had elected to lie on the grass, with paws neatly spread before the chest, in the attidude of the sphinx. I saw all the cats, a considerable number, of whom quite a large proportion were Siamese, and none appeared unhappy; all were rather plump! Clearly they cannot in kennels run as they would like to do; but no cats could have looked so contented, had such fine coats, nor been so plump if they had not been properly fed and looked after.

You can, in Britain, arrange to have your cat moved from one quarantine station to another if you were not satisfied. If you wished to import a cat from any place other than Ireland, the Channel Islands or the Isle of Man, you must first secure a place in one of the approved quarantine stations; and then engage an authorized carrying agent to meet your cat at its port of arrival. Full details of quarantine stations and carrying agents can be obtained from the Ministry of Agriculture, Fisheries and Food, Animal Health Division; or, in Scotland, from the Department of Agriculture and Fisheries. Having secured a place and an agent, you then apply to the Ministry for a licence, which will be sent to the agent so that he can clear your cat (or dog) through the customs. The animal is taken, under quarantine conditions, i.e. in a muzzle-proof and paw-proof crate, to his destination. Removal to another quarantine station is carried out in the same manner and with a fresh licence, so it is obviously always best to see for yourself where your animal is going before making final arrangements. Quarantine is not a cheap business; you pay £30 a month, and the quarantine period at present (1977) is six months. Circumstances may lessen or increase the length of the quarantine period in force, and inflation, as in all matters, may affect prices.[4] It is interesting that some time ago every animal had to go into a separate compartment whereas recently, two belonging to the same person could be lodged together provided the owner agreed that if one proved to have rabies, both should be destroyed.

Australia has the most severe quarantine laws of any country—which is easily understood since she has always been concerned with huge herds of cattle. A cat sent to Australia even from a rabies-free country must travel in quarantine conditions, and will be put into kennels at the station nearest to his port of entry: there is no choice at all for the owner. However, conditions are so good and the cats so well cared-for that complaints seem never to be made. The Australians dearly love their pets but they, with both feet firmly planted on the ground and all the commonsense in the world, are not likely to sentimentalize to the extent of playing against loaded dice. I have recently (1977) returned from a judging tour in Australia and New Zealand, and in Perth, Western Australia, I saw the new quarantine station. This is a very big place, splendidly appointed: the kitchens are a model, and there are excellent arrangements for veterinary attention. In the section devoted to cats the little prisoners were in a grand shape—as indeed were such dogs as I had time to see. No one need be afraid to send his cat or kitten here, where every precaution is taken, and all attention is given.

New Zealand will accept cats from the British Isles without any quarantine on arrival provided the cat can be shown to have been nine months in Britain; and Jamaica will accept, with free entry, those who have been six months in Britain. America has no quarantine laws and there 2,348 cases of rabies occurred in the first six months of 1967. In Europe there were over 5,000 recorded cases in that year; but here a quarantine policy would be quite impracticable because of the land frontiers: no use, for instance, to impose quarantine in Switzerland where a rabid animal may walk in without let or hindrance from France, Italy or Germany. On the continent of Europe vaccination is extensively used; it does not offer complete protection, but it may help to reduce the incidence of the disease. In Britain, where rabies is not endemic and where there are protective laws, it would be absurd to insist upon the inoculation of every dog and cat with a vaccine which is not a hundred per cent effective. But obviously in countries where quarantine is not possible, vaccination is better than nothing.

It appears that in Canada, skunks are carriers of this disease; and in zoos lions may be so. Zoo animals brought to Britain have always undergone a suitable period of quarantine. The incubation period for rabies is at least four months. Six months have hitherto been rare; but there have been cases which have become manifest after six months, though until 1969 always while the affected animals were still in quarantine kennels. 'The incidence of rabies continues to increase throughout the world and the disease has recently become more widespread in countries in western Europe'.[3] The British have, by stringently enforced laws, kept their shores free of this terrible illness, so menacing to man and beast alike. Experienced people have always held the opinion that if the laws were rescinded, there would be rabies rife in Britain within a twelvemonth. The truth of this has been brought home to all concerned by this appearance of the disease in 1969-70. No owner of a Siamese cat who has given thought to the matter could doubt that the Minister made a right decision. Where this condition is concerned, it is vitally important that we should never let ourselves be lulled into an amnesia which can be nothing but a false sense of security. If, in these days of big populations, human, canine and feline, we sow seeds of laxity in this respect, we shall reap a truly frightful harvest. But within the shelter of their good laws, their customs efficiency and their sea barrier, the quarantine countries can be safe from this scourge: they, and all their pets, not least the cats with the pale coats and the coloured-points.

### MOTHERLESS KITTENS

It is, fortunately, not very often that a queen dies while her kittens are very young; but it can happen. The hazards of the road are always with us; and it has more than once happened that a Siamese queen has died of illness caused by sepsis due to a wound—in one case, a torn nipple. Such an unhappy situation leaves the breeder with the problem of saving the kittens. The ideal is a foster-mother, but it is not always possible to find one. What is wanted is a healthy queen who has a very small litter of her own or whose owner does not want any kittens and intends to keep only one for his queen's benefit. As can be imagined, such an animal is not so easily acquired as, say, a loaf if the household is short of bread! It is a good idea to tell the Royal Society, the Cat's Protection League, the Police, the neighbouring vet.-surgeons and everybody you know from the milkman to the bank manager. You never know who could have heard of a suitable queen, and news travels; the more people know, the better.

The kittens' need is *immediate*; it is necessary at once to feed them with a dropper. The best thing to give them is warm (not boiled) cow's milk, not from the top of the bottle, with a little water and some caster sugar added. If they are less than a fortnight old, the task of feeding them is almost a wholetime job; fortunate indeed is the breeder who has another queen with a litter, and so can let the kittens take turns at being with the mother, and supplement her milk by hand-feeding. If there is no such fortunate situation, then it is a great blessing if more than one person in a household can help with hand-feeding; for a kitten of a week or less must feed more or less continuously to survive. At a fortnight, the work is easier and the chances better: two-hourly feeds may be given and, if the kittens are healthy and are good 'do-ers', they will thrive. It is astonishing how eagerly they will suck from a dropper, recognising the person who feeds them and greeting him with eager cries of anticipation. Whereas some individuals can be weakly, yet Siamese kittens who are healthy will, given half-a-chance, live. At first, they need to be fed round the clock, but the poor exhausted owner, even if he be doing the work by himself and with no help at all, will have the reward of seeing them grow. They will quickly climb up on to him if he sits on the floor to feed them, and will appear mildly surprised that only one can feed at a time. It soon becomes possible to give only one feed during the night, and if the dish be left on the floor at mealtimes, it is astonishing how soon the kittens will discover where the milk comes from, and start to take it for themselves. Before they are three weeks old, they will probably all be taking milk from the dish—and this, of course, is a great relief to the tired owner. But is has a drawback!

Normally, kittens will think about finely-chopped solid food at between three and four weeks, and will take milk, unless their dam has a poor supply, somewhat later; at four weeks or maybe more they will stand round a dish of milk, lapping it. But tiny kittens, deprived of their dam and finding the dish at, perhaps, not much more than a fortnight old, take it as they would take their mother's milk; feeding from her, they would be lying down, on a blanket, against her 'waistcoat', even on her flank—but always lying face-down against the life-giving supplies. Losing her, and being hand-fed, they seize eagerly upon the dropper, sucking vigorously and clinging to the person giving them food: spread-eagled, always, against the source of supply. When they find the dish, they start at once to suck in, and then to lap, the milk; but to get at it in what at their age is the normal manner, they lie face-down in the dish! It does not last long; a few days, and they are standing and lapping, and accepting tiny bits of beef or cooked rabbit; but until then, it is necessary to wash them over with warm water and dry them off with a heated towel after every meal! There is great joy in finding that their lives are saved, and a kitten so reared will never forget the person who fostered him: years later he will, just now and then, cling to his owner, clawing, purring, and sucking for a brief few minutes the neck of the human who saved his life.

It is a good thing to have a periodic check on the teeth: many a Siamese has lived to a ripe old age because teeth that were carious had been removed in good time.

GERIATRICS

Old age, for a Siamese cat, is around 15 or 16 years; some have lived longer, others, as with all species, have lost their lives young. When a cat becomes really old, there will be a slowing-down of his usual activities; he will go out less, eat less and more slowly, spend a lot of his time asleep. He may need attention—perhaps regular doses of liquid paraffin, maybe more grooming than of yore, and some 'flea-powder' rubbed into his coat. So long as he is well and contented, he can live his life out as a pensioner with just a small amount of extra care; and with a little bit of good fortune, he may travel in his sleep to the happy hunting grounds.

## Chapter six

# Breeding and stud work

Stud work is by far the most exacting aspect of breeding. It carries a very heavy responsibility, and it gives to the stud owner almost from the start the anxiety of keeping the cat in separate quarters.

It is impossible to have a full male living in the house with his owner; he will 'spray' walls and furniture and, other damage apart, the odour will be most unpleasant. This is his nature and no blame attaches to him: however sweet his disposition, he cannot be at one and the same time a whole male and a pet. The owner may have bred him, or bought him, intending from the start to keep his as a stud. Having been selected for this work, he will be an extremely beautiful cat, perhaps one of the year's winning Siamese kittens, and he may have a very affectionate disposition; but the moment will come when he must be put outside the house, to live in his own quarters. There has been at least one contrary opinion on this matter. In a Siamese Cat Club *News Sheet* of nearly 30 years ago Violet Dawson, at that time honorary secretary to the Western Provinces Cat Club, Cape Town, South Africa, gives her views and states that her own stud has the run of the countryside as well as of the house; she considers that spraying is a temporary habit which disappears, and writes that her stud used to come home scratched and bitten when he was young, but never after reaching adulthood. The vast majority of stud owners will not agree with this opinion on spraying; moreover, whereas a young adult male running free will win his battles, when he becomes older it will be his turn to be defeated and, maybe, badly hurt. In any case this lady would, very likely, keep a male cat enclosed nowadays, if only because of the ever-growing risk of the road.

### STUD QUARTERS

A stud-house, to be really suitable for its purpose, ought to be well-

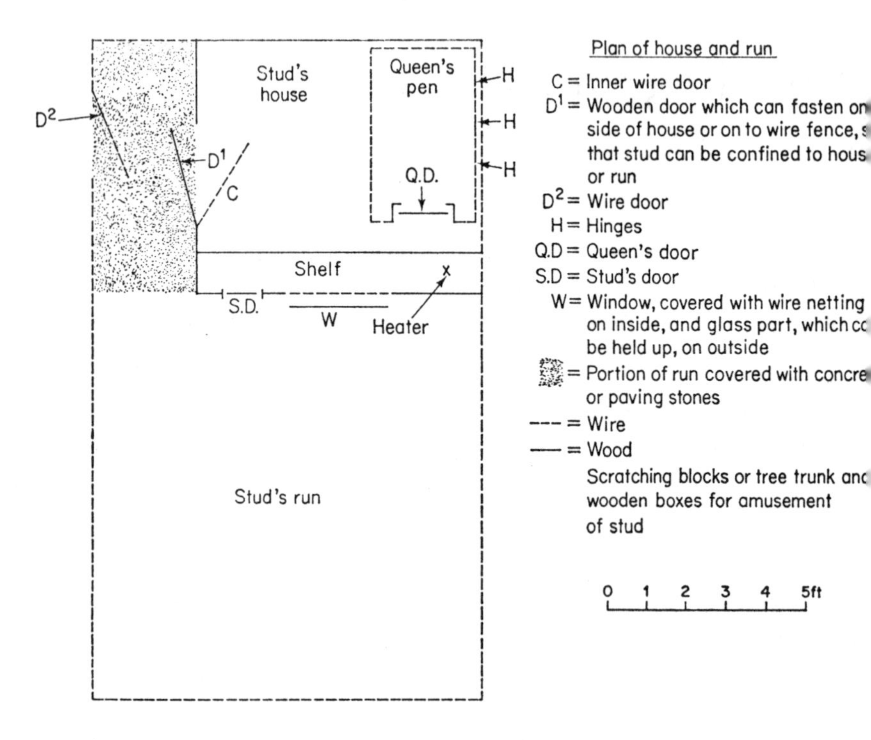


A STUD HOUSE

1. Stud house must be not less than 6ft 6ins high at highest end and 5ft 6ins at lowest end. It should be lined, with a washable surface, to conserve the heat.

2. The upper part of the stud house wall next to the run should have a 4ft 6ins wide window, the centre part of which opens.

3. The heater may be tubular or free standing, and should be situated under the shelf at the end opposite the stud's door. It should be fixed so that it cannot be knocked down and cause fire.

4. The stud's run should be as large as possible.

5. Both large doors, D¹ and D² should have outer and inner fastenings.

6. The queen's pen should be collapsible so that it can be removed, 2ft 6ins high, with walls of wire netting, opening at the top with hinges next to the stud wall.

built, warm, and to have access to a 'garden' of its own. These are minimum requirements; if there is not enough ground to provide an enclosed space for fresh air and exercise, it is better not to keep a stud. Some people have brick-built out-houses which can be made into good stud quarters, but very nice pre-fabricated wooden houses, sizable and raised from the ground, can be obtained from manufacturers of cat accessories. In winter, artificial heating is necessary —at any rate at night; and it is essential to instal a perfectly safe method of heating. It must always be a bad thing to 'coddle' a Siamese, but a stud is not able to take much exercise and, despite his excellent fur coat and leggings, he may feel cold on a winter night. There is a wide choice of heating arrangements: some owners put in an enclosed oil-stove, clamped to the floor so that it cannot be knocked over; some favour electric strip-heating, installed at such a height that the cat cannot reach it. Some stud-houses are built against the owner's own house, so that whatever central heating is used may be guided to the stud quarters. In the present age of rapid technical improvements, new ways of achieving warmth in catteries must constantly come onto the market, and a heating system can be out-of-date almost overnight. Warm blankets of course, will have to be provided, and there must be a good sleeping place. Cats like to be 'up', and a shelf, a raised 'cupboard', a basket on legs—any of these will contribute to the cat's comfort when the time comes to put him outside—always a sad moment for those who cherished him as a kitten.

There is no real reason why a stud should always be lonely; those who undertake stud work are people devoted to the males, and they very often keep more than one at stud. This usually means more than one stud-house; for two male Siamese cats to get on well together is the exception rather than the rule, although it can happen. In the late 1940s there were two famous male cats, father and son, one a seal-point and one a blue-point, who lived together in perfect amity. Admittedly, they had a very large enclosure and a big house with rows of comfortable shelves and little inner 'rooms' where they could be put with visiting queens: even the presence of a queen for one of them did not make them quarrel. But such a situation is unusual! However, in many of the larger catteries a stud will be able to see other cats—perhaps a queen and her kittens in the enclosure next to his. And in very many cases he will have a queen or queens of his own, who can share his isolation and be company for him. Without some companionship he could be a very lonely cat, for visiting queens may be few and far between, and indeed this is one of the problems and anxieties which stud owners have to face: too many queens would be bad for their male, and so also would too few. In addition to which, he is an expensive proposition. The bills for his food, for heating, for the upkeep of his quarters and for advertising his prowess are not inconsiderable and, unless he has plenty of visiting queens during the year, he will be an expensive luxury. Some studs attain immediate popularity; a male who is a good example of a new variety will be greatly in demand; a cat who has become a champion and won best-in-show awards may expect a successful career; a male with a reputation for siring good litters will have plenty of little brides. But his owner will still have many anxieties.

To take a cat round to championship shows in the hope of getting the necessary three challenge certificates which will make him a champion is nerve-wracking to say the least; how many owners of beautiful, successful kittens have decided to keep them for stud and have entered them in Open classes at championship shows only to find, when they had penned their really beautiful boy, that there was in the class a rival who quite obviously would rate just those two or three marks more that would get him the precious certificate? And supposing the boy is the best, and the judge awards the challenge certificate? Off he goes to another show, to try to collect a second under another judge, and the poor owner's heart is in his mouth, he is hoping and praying, and even if all goes well there is still that third challenge certificate to be hoped for and longed for.

Indeed some cats have never got the third certificate that would have made them champions. But a really fine specimen will, barring accidents, achieve championship status, and start upon his career as a stud cat. Then for the owner comes the expenditure of money for advertising in suitable journals, show catalogues and so on, and of energy in keeping the boy and his quarters perfectly clean. It all sounds simple enough but, in fact, if you have more than one stud, a great deal of hard work is needed to see to their meals and to attend to the cleaning and upkeep of their houses; there is always worry lest the cats should get too little work; and the need to keep a queen or so on the premises for their benefit, thus making more chores. It is, indeed, practically impossible for one person to look after more than one stud cat properly; when two people, or even a family, live together and are interested in cats, the work is easy because it is shared; when someone wishes to keep several cats and can afford to employ and to house cattery attendants—well and good. But for one person—someone whose family maybe does not share his or her love of cats—it is best not to have too many; the owner has only to be ill for a week or so—and the cats are inevitably neglected to some extent.

Of course, there are people, maybe a husband and wife, who work together in one household to look after a cattery, and these, as a rule, are the successful stud owners, the ones who can at any moment display with pride to any unexpected visitor their champion stud and his beautifully kept quarters.

## VISITING QUEENS

Even for them, it is anxious work to look after visiting queens. Those who love cats can enjoy the paper-work and telephoning that precedes a visit, but to take charge of someone else's beloved queen must always be a responsibility. Someone will bring her, or the stud-owner will undertake to meet her at station or airport; sometimes there can be a technical hitch; it is anguish for all concerned if the queen be late or, as has happened on railways, be mislaid. With care this need not happen, and she can usually be taken to her prospective groom quietly and quickly.

Since there are no two Siamese cats alike, the stud owner will know what to expect of his cat but not, unless he is already acquainted with her, how the queen is likely to behave. If she is the male's first queen, the owner will have had weeks of worry as to whether his wonderful boy is in fact mature; he will not even be able to advertise the male as a stud until he has been proved. Sometimes a good, strong, healthy male will, for no apparent reason, be a very St Anthony. Queens of experience have been put with such cats—queens who were to be trusted to remain gentle; queens who have done their seductive best, rolling and crooling to the bashful male—to no avail. Be it said, such shy cats usually come to maturity in no uncertain manner—better late than never; but their long immaturity must always be an irritation to the owner. Alternatively, the owner of a Siamese cattery may get a surprise: one such who had a calling queen whom he did not immediately want mated, felt sorry for her, shut up alone, and put a four-months old male kitten in with her for company. The kitten was not shy. . . .

The owner of a proved stud needs to provide a space in the stud-house where the queen can be enclosed, for she may be angry, and hurt the boy. There are various ways of arranging this, including the purchase of a 'queen-cage'—a small, netted run; an important point is that there should be an escape-route for the male. For the queen may become ill-tempered. The stud is not likely to harm her for no one could keep at stud a cat who was at all vicious; but the queen, subject to unaccustomed pressures and finding herself in strange surroundings could, in a sort of love-hate temper, really hurt him. This is unusual, but it may be evident in a maiden queen. Experienced queens known to be gentle and easy to woo are many, and queens either too vicious to be with the stud or too nervous to be mated are the exception; but with a new visitor, it is the stud owner's job to find out what she is like before leaving her with the male. As a rule, nature will, as usual, take care of things; one stud owner telephoned the people who had sent their queen and said 'I can't get her mated; I shall have to send her back—what can I do?' 'Shut them in,' came the reply 'and send her back in the morning.' She had fine kittens.

It is important that the queen be sent early when she calls; this is for her owner to see to; it will greatly help the stud owner if she does not arrive too late. A maiden queen is not necessarily difficult. I can recall a very young queen with the prettiest imaginable ways who, crooling gently, curled into a writhing ball on the floor, put her arms over her face, and peered over them with sparkling blue eyes. The stud owner was asked whether, being a maiden, she had been awkward to deal with; it appeared she had walked in, kissed her groom, and been mated within five minutes.

### LITTER CLASSES

It is a matter of moment to a stud's career that he should sire good litters. At some shows there are classes for best stud cat and best brood queen, and competitors are judged on their progeny. A stud will compete, obviously, only if his owner knows that some of his kittens have also been entered, in a litter class. There will be more work for a boy known to sire strong, beautiful kittens and, if possible, big litters. This last is, in fact, not relevant, for there is

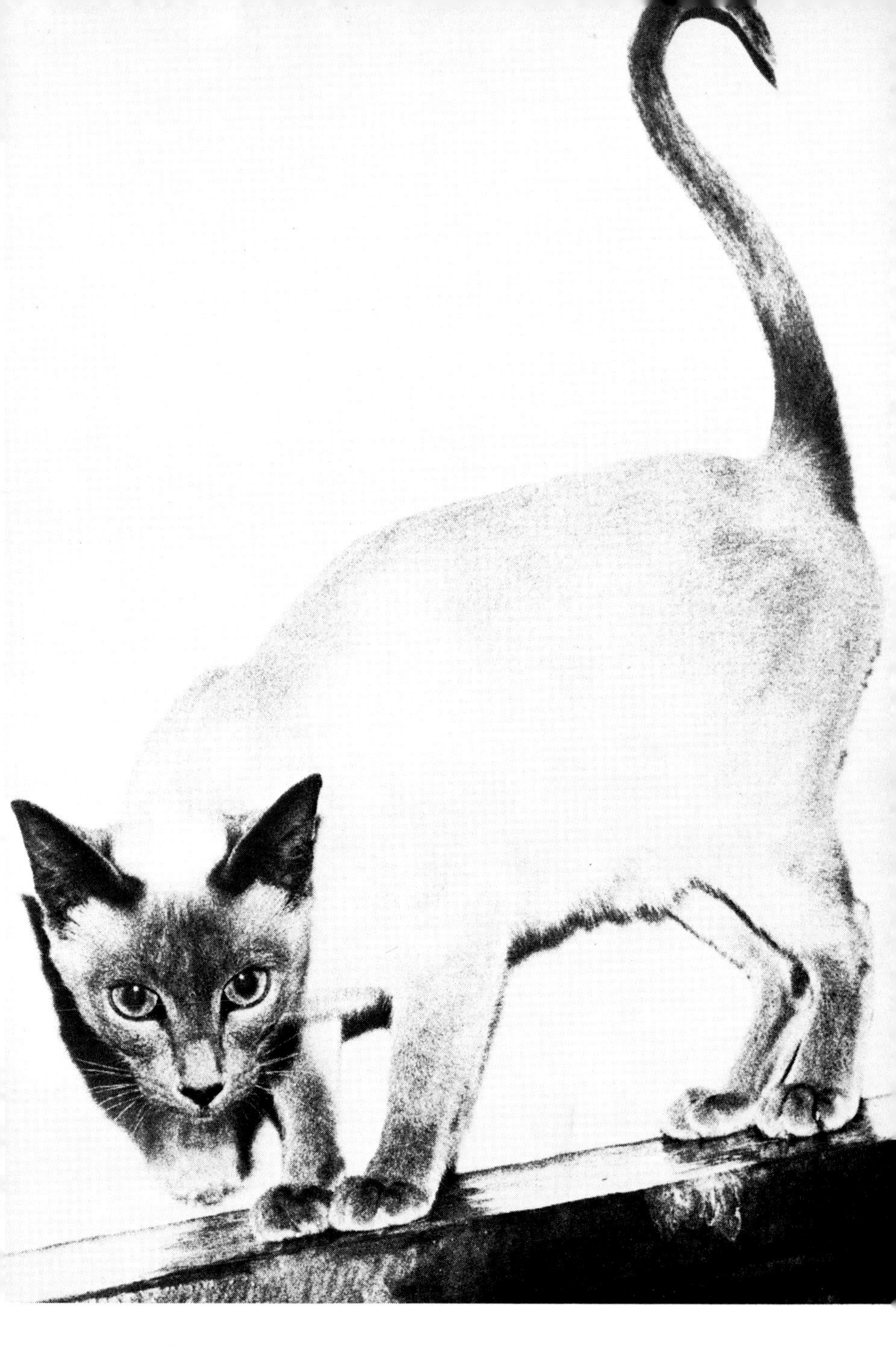

17 Female blue-point "Flamma v. Monte Bisbino", owned and bred by Mme. E Witschi of Caneggio, Switzerland

18 Blue-point stud "Ona Lopez", owned by Mrs Burlton, Gerrards Cross, Buckinghamshire, England

19 Champion blue-point stud "Blue Beau", owned by Mrs S Smith of Thurleigh, Bedfordshire, England

20 Premier blue-point neuter "Chicabu", owned by Mrs Lait of Wolverhampton, England

21 Blue-point, owned by Mrs Johnson of Hampstead, London, showing well its pale coat

22 Grand Champion "Che-Ree's Tao" of Webb-Barr, bred by Sherrie-Joseph F Bender and owned by Mrs Eleanor T Webb of Havre de Grace, Maryland, USA

Champion lilac-point "Nokomis
Domino" bred by Mrs Maloney
Mr Scott of Melbourne, Australia
owned by Mrs Proud of Auckland,
Zealand

Grand Champion "April in Paris", a
le lilac-point bred and owned by
e Page of Lake View Terrace,
ornia, USA

25 "Burdach Naattiffe", a female owned by Mrs.V Gane of Shipston Stour, Warwickshire, England

26 Red-point kitten "Asuni Pyewacket" at play with seal-point "Quintral Calypso" watching. Ow Mrs Abbey of Burnham, Buckinghamshire, England

27 Lilac-point "Quintral Pettifleur" with kittens. Owner: Mrs Abbey

28 Lilac-point kitten "Pintra Blue Boy", belonging to Mrs S Roberts of Ashby-de-la-Zouch, Leicestershire, England

nothing in the stud to govern the size of a litter; but it is hard to persuade the general public of this, though it is, really, just a simple matter of the mechanics of reproduction. In Siamese, an average litter will consist of five kittens, and a litter of four or five may be accepted as normal. For there to be six or more, or only three or less, is unusual, and it is reasonable for the breeder whose queen produces litters of unusual size to be interested in knowing why. Taking five as the average, some are inclined to say that a litter of small size is the 'fault' of the sire or dam. Well, if we are dealing with normalcy, we can eliminate the sire at once. It is of course true that you can have a male cat who is sterile. The causes of sterility range from genetic factors to accidents. Everybody knows by now that if—unusual in itself!—a tortoiseshell-pointed male should appear, he is inevitably sterile: as discussed in chapter 2 it has just recently been discovered that this is because of a genetic imbalance due to the presence in such a cat of two X chromosomes instead of the usual one, as well as a Y. In fact, there are many reasons, physical and hereditary, why a cat, male or female, may be sterile or may have kittens which are not viable. Given a normal pair, however, the ova will be fertilized, the queen will duly kitten, and the number of her kittens will have nothing to do with the sire, for, as any biologist will say, there is nothing in him to govern the size of the litter. This is easily understood if you realize that when a mating takes place, millions of spermatazoa are aimed at the ova; nature with survival as her only goal, is very lavish. If the stud be sterile, as can happen, then conception will not take place. Assuming him to be a normal, fertile cat, then it is ridiculous to suppose that in a species where the average litter consists of five, only one or two of the sperms that find their mark are capable of fertilizing the ova.

With the queen, it is another matter; size of litters may be governed by the age of the dam. She may be very young; sometimes a queen will call so persistently that it becomes necessary to get her mated before she is full-grown. Many a cat is not full size until, maybe, 15 months; in such a case, the litter may easily be below the normal size—perhaps three, or even only two kittens; there will very likely be a normal-sized litter in the following year. The dam may be very old: in England there have recently appeared in the national press pictures of a beautiful longhair tabby, aged 24 years, with her one kitten! At such an age, she was a grand girl to kitten at all!

### SIZE OF LITTERS

Numbers in a litter may also be governed by the size of the queen. This is not invariably true; there are small, elegant Siamese queens who habitually have litters of five kittens. But size is nevertheless a possible factor; a particularly small female may always produce litters of three, or at most four, kittens; and an exceptionally big queen is likely to be the one to have litters of six or more kittens. During the war, I had a raking great seal-pointed girl of impeccable ancestry and strong character who produced litters of six or seven; however there was, at about the same time, a cat of no enormous size who had eight kittens and reared them all with ease. Nature's object is, of couse, survival; her principle is that life must go on. And in furtherance of her aims, she has so arranged matters that the smallest mammalia, the ones most easily preyed upon, shall have the shortest gestation period and the biggest families. Thus cat is likely to eat mouse, so mouse has frequent and large litters in order that plenty will have a chance to survive, and the genus will go on. So it goes throughout; the large elephant, not likely to have many predators, has a gestation of almost two years, and one at a birth; man, well able to look after himself, nine months and, normally, one offspring; cat, with, in the wild, many predators, just over two months and an average litter of five—so as to be sure that some will survive and carry on the race. All the same, nature, still anxious for survival, is careful not to ask the impossible: if a small, or very young queen be mated, then she may well have the small litter that she will be capable of carrying and rearing. There are always exceptions: the young queen who comes up with six very fine kittens, the Siamese who failed to win because she was too big, and then produced a mere three or four kits!

It will, however, rebound to the stud's credit if he is known to have sired litters of six or seven, especially with the breeder who thinks in terms of money, and therefore desires his queens to have very large litters. There are, alas, people who when their queens kitten count up the number of new arrivals and say to themselves 'That will be so many dollars'. This is in fact a foolish point of view, you can run a battery of hens or a pig-farm as a profit-making business, but the same rules will not apply to pet animals. The hens and the pigs provide food for human sustenance, and there is always a market for this: keep the birds and the animals in the right conditions, and you can reckon on a successful trading proposition. Breeding pets is a different thing altogether. For these there is only ever a limited market, and there are always the dictates of fashion. Fashion has, for years now, greatly favoured the Siamese cat; but it is still not possible to rear kittens on a large scale and expect to find a ready market. Breeders are up against the quirks of the fancy, too. Raise a lot of fine fat pigs, and those dealing in bacon will be interested; but the purchaser of Siamese probably wants just one kitten, and may insist upon one whose parents have won championships! There is no doubt that by the time a breeder has carted his cats around to various shows; has paid for good food for them and laid out money on proper housing and heating; has had, maybe, a bad season with illness and vet.-surgeon's bills, he will be lucky indeed to break even.

Breeding pet animals is, in fact, a luxury hobby; but it can give enormous interest and pleasure to the person who loves the creatures concerned. And it is certainly love of the cats which makes people undertake the onerous duties of caring properly for stud cats. It has often happened that after a very successful career as a stud, the owner will neuter the cat, who, after all, cannot be used indefinitely since most fanciers know better than to inbreed too closely. Retirement will certainly please the cat! An owner of years ago, taking her neutered boy back into the house, said 'He is so happy!'

### BREEDING QUEENS

A breeding queen, of course, can be a house pet as well, provided the owner is prepared to watch carefully for signs that she may be thinking romantic thoughts: no serious breeder wants what Lady Arkell, who was one of the chocolate-point breeders of the late 1940s always referred to as 'illegities'. However, if a mis-mating should occur, it is important to leave the dam one kitten, even if the rest are to be destroyed; if all her kittens are taken from a healthy queen, she will be wretched, and it will not be good for her and may, indeed, lead to a mastitis from milk which she cannot get rid of.

People who decide to start breeding Siamese very often already have a friend in the fancy who will give them all the advice they need. For a beginner who has fallen in love with the breed and wishes to join in and be a breeder himself, it is a good idea to go to two or three shows and to note which are the winners, and why.

Despite the eager desire to possess a kitten, it is much best not to be rushed into buying one. In looking at the exhibits at a show, it is easy to get into conversation with other people, since most of the folk present will share a common interest. Some of those with whom you can make acquaintance may be the breeders of the cats who have done well, and some may be judges of the breed, or hold some official position or other. It is still best not to be in too great a hurry. A proper price to pay for a queen kitten to be bred from is £60; in America maybe $400 if she is of top quality. Established breeders who offer a kitten to a novice are as often as not knowledgeable, genuine and in every way honest; but, just now and then, as in every walk of life, the tyro may meet someone who is not quite honest or who can himself be mistaken as to the quality of a kitten. It is best to go slowly: if a kitten is offered who is the sister of a best-in-show winner, she may be just what is wanted—and she may not. It does not do to be 'panicked' by the fear of missing something good. Perhaps this kitten is very good indeed, but there will be others; much best to hold-your-horses and become really well-acquainted with the cats and with the fancy; and certainly best to start with only one queen.

If only one queen is involved, it is easier to learn the ins-and-outs of breeding. To start with too many is to multiply the difficulties and hazards which of necessity beset the novice. The beginner who starts to breed Siamese will find things difficult if he thinks he knows it all; and yet it may happen that his friends in the fancy will shower him with too much advice. Probably the best way is to start with a little basic knowledge, and then proceed with simple commonsense; for most of the problems earnestly discussed can be settled by commonsense alone. Having said that if something is obviously wrong then veterinary advice must be sought, the rest can be left to nature and to ordinary 'horse sense'.

## CALLING QUEENS

It is when the queen starts calling, at nine months give or take a week or so, that the excitement and pleasure of breeding, as well as its difficulties, will start. It is a good thing to have a boy lined up for her beforehand: he can be chosen from advertisements in, for instance, in Britain, *Fur and Feather*, which is the official organ of the Governing Council of the Cat Fancy, or his services may be arranged for in good time through a friendship made at a show or through a club; Stud lists are kept by governing bodies all over the world, and club secretaries will always advise anyone who wishes to buy a copy. It is not a bad idea to hold a queen back for her first call which may, in any case, be a weak one, especially if she came into season very young. She will probably not be completely full-grown until she is over a year old, and it is therefore better for her not to kitten too young. However, she may force the owner's hand: if she calls without cessation for a very long time, or calls for a week, stops for a week, calls again—and so on, in a ceaseless stop-go cycle, then something must be done about it; for her own sake since she may call herself thin, and for the owner's sake, who will be deafened by her incessant shouting. Any other cat will emit only a plaintive 'mew' or, as in a Burmese, a firm little 'Miaow' of protest; but a Siamese queen in season has to be heard to be believed, and if it becomes necessary to calm her, it is well to have arranged matters with the owner of a suitable stud beforehand.

Sometimes a queen mated for the first time will not 'take', and the stud owner will usually give another service if he be notified within five weeks. Usually, however, the queen will be in kitten, and it will be necessary to give her plenty of extra food during her pregnancy, which will be of approximately 68 days. It is well to keep the queen shut up for a few days after her return from stud, for she may not have completed her call, and may meet with a stray tom in the garden. The arrival of the kittens is not generally anything to be afraid of, but it is possible for matters to go wrong. It is best to know the telephone number of your vet. and to be sure that he will give an emergency night service if needed. The time to be worried is the time when the queen is having strong contractions without result. There may be a breech presentation, or a kitten with the neck presenting; it takes skill to push the unborn kitten back between contractions and draw the head forward as a fresh contraction starts; it may be that a bad presentation will need a caesarian section. It is necessary to have qualified help if the queen is in distress; and it is better, if you feel that all is not well, to send for help in the daytime or in the evening than to wait until the middle of the night.

KITTENING

But as a rule, her kittens will arrive quickly and she will deal expeditiously with the matter of tidying up. It is not at all unusual, even with the first litter, for the owner to leave a queen in labour, and to return well within an hour to find that she has three or four kittens, all beautifully washed and polished, lying in a neat row feeding voraciously; often there is hardly a stain on the blanket. It is not, however, wise to leave a queen in labour for long; she may require her owner to take a kitten, wrapping it in a warmed towel, while she deals with the next arrival. Her new kittens will be a great joy to her; she will lie in a sort of ecstasy kneading the air above them and purring loudly enough to be heard from quite a distance. She will require constant supplies of fresh food, milk and water, for only so can she rear a successful litter. The kittens will be no trouble at all at first, but when they are three or maybe four weeks old, they will start to eat for themselves.

It is a mistake to look for trouble, especially when it is non-existent. The weaning of kittens for instance is endlessly talked about: At what age should they be weaned? Ought they to be removed from their dam, and how should she be treated to ensure that there is not too much milk? What food should be offered to the kittens, and what should be done to encourage them to lap? And a great many more questions and the answer to most of them is 'Nonsense'! A Siamese is not, basically, very different from any other cat; admittedly, he has that endearing love of human companionship which is such a joy to cat lovers. But when it comes to the ordinary cycle of reproduction, feline behaviour follows a pattern; and so long as we realize that the pattern varies a little within well-defined limits, we shall have a fair idea of what to expect. A brood queen who is well fed can go on feeding her kittens for longer than can a queen unsuitably or inadequately fed. A queen with a small litter can, properly nourished, nurse them for longer than one with six or seven kittens. If your brood queen looks thin and wretched, offer solid food to the kittens; if the kittens squeal and cry, offer them food. All these things are a matter of commonsense.

FEEDING KITTENS

Normally, kittens will start to show some interest in solid food at about three or four weeks; it can be later, if their dam's milk is rich and plentiful: so long as their natural food is sufficiently sustaining, they will tend to stick with it. On the other hand, if the dam's milk is poor in quality or inadequate in quantity, the kittens will look for something better. It is easy for the owner to see if they are too thin, or are not satisfied with what they are getting. People will sometimes say that they want to wean kittens in order to sell them, or in order to exhibit the queen; these are not good reasons. There are, on the other hand, excellent reasons for not weaning them—always provided that the maternal supplies are adequate. One is their natural immunity to undesirable organisms: they are less likely to be ill while they are being nursed for they will have immunity from their dam. Another is that the queen is not so likely to call while she is feeding her kittens. This is not an invariable rule, but by-and-large it holds good. A well-known breeder says that she realizes that kittens need to be weaned when they start to show interest in what is offered to their dam. Personally, I offer very finely-chopped raw beef at between three and four weeks. It is always refused but I offer it once a day; in due course, one member of the party will sniff at the dish, lick the meat, and finally take some—after which the others soon come to see what he has found that is so good! No matter how well-cared-for the queen may be, it must, after a month, become a strain for her to feed kittens which, because they are growing, will require ever more and more nourishment. Provided the kittens are well, it is no use trying to force the pace. Put down something for them: if they do not want it, the mother will finish it up; but in due course they will start eating. If they seem slow to take food, put tiny bits in their mouths—it is often a pleasant surprise to them! One thing not always appreciated by beginners is that it is no use offering cow's milk to kittens who are still getting supplies from their dam; they are getting what for them is the best possible drink. But solids are another matter; tiny bits of boiled fish, boiled rabbit or raw beef—these are tit-bits that their dam cannot supply, and fast-growing kittens will soon recognize their worth.

It is never necessary to worry about small discrepancies; a fat kitten who starts eating late; a big litter of kittens who start early—these are nothing to perturb the breeder. So long as the feline family is in good health, nature will take care of them. Sometimes, they will go on for weeks taking milk from their dam as well as devouring large meals, even as well as drinking plenty of cow's milk. Gradually, it will sort itself out.

### NEW-BORN KITTENS

It must be remembered that Siamese kittens are born white (see Chapter 5). The gene for restriction-of-colour-to-points is connected with the temperature mechanism, so that the colour can show only at the cooler extremities. In utero, the kitten is too warm for colour to show at all, but it will begin to appear a few days after their birth. Those beautiful blue eyes, too, are not quite like the eyes of other kittens who, arriving with their eyes shut, are always said to be 'born blind'. The eyes of Siamese kittens open shortly after they are born—sometimes they are half-open at birth, and they will become 'sticky' if the kittens are allowed to be in a bright light; the light in their room should always be veiled for the first ten days of their lives. They will, unless they are ill, always be perfectly clean; when they start eating, a shallow scratch-tray should be provided, and the kittens will always use it. Many things are used to fill scratch-trays; peat-moss, the manufactured items produced by well-known firms, even torn-up newspaper. It is not a bad idea to provide ordinary garden or orchard soil, which is what would naturally be used by cats, keeping always a bag of peat-moss or some such substitute for use on wet days; but earth is not always available to those who live in towns, and the cats take very kindly to whatever suitable alternative is provided.

### REGISTRATION

It will be necessary to register the kittens with the governing body concerned—in Britain, the Governing Council of the Cat Fancy; and the address to which to write for a form may be found on the transfer-of-ownership certificate. The vendor should have provided a transfer form, duly signed, for the queen's new owner to fill up and send off with a small fee, and in return, a new form certifying the change will have arrived; on it will be the name and address of the Registrar who can always provide forms for registration of new kittens. The importance of registration lies in the impossibility of showing unless the exhibit has duly been registered under the rules of the governing body concerned; and of the unwillingness of most people to buy an unregistered kitten. A copy of the pedigree, written out and given to a purchaser but lacking a registration number has little value. Anyone can write out a pedigree and most people will write it quite correctly; but the presence of the registration number on the copy means that the new owner can, if he wishes, and on sending a fee to the registrar, obtain confirmation of its accuracy. It is a guarantee of the kitten's ancestry. In Britain the letters S.R. attached to the registration number stand for supplementary register, and quite a few people think that some sort of disgrace attaches to this. In fact they are mistaken, since the supplementary register is for cats and kittens not yet showing three generations of like breeding behind them. Thus, the first lilac-points to be bred were entered in the supplementary register; later, when a kitten arrived whose parents, four grandparents and eight great-grandparents were all lilac-points, his or her name was duly inscribed in the full register; but no stigma attaches to the very first 'lilacs'. The register is a record, not a list of class distinctions. (See chapter 9).

## IMMUNIZATION

An absolute 'must' is inoculation, as mentioned in Chapter 5. The many vaccines evolved during the last thirty years or so are for immunization against FIE, feline infectious enteritis; this condition of the intestine is really frightful, and vaccination assuredly protects from it. Since first I used the Graueb vaccine in the early 1940s no cat of mine has had either feline infectious enteritis or the condition known as cat 'flu; this may be fortuitous; I have become inclined to believe that cat 'flu is a respiratory form of the same distemper; but the manufacturers of the vaccines state categorically that they are a protection against FIE—they claim no more than this. The latest vaccine used, Katavac, is expensive; each kitten pays a high price for his 'jab'; in Britain, £3.50; but it confers a long-lasting immunity, so that it is not necessary to give frequent 'booster' inoculations.

## BUYING AND SELLING

When the kittens are registered and duly immunized, there comes the business of finding suitable homes for them. Sometimes they will have been booked even before birth by other breeders interested in their pedigrees, or by friends; more often than not, they must be advertised. Obviously, there is a wide choice of advertising media—from official periodicals and show catalogues (if you have outstanding kittens and wish to announce the fact to other fanciers) through country journals and the dailies, to your local press. The last is particularly useful if you hope that your kittens may become neutered pets in really kind homes. A kitten obviously in championship class and to be used for breeding ought not to be sold for less than £60 ($400); for a Siamese sold to be a neutered pet, as little as £25 may be asked. But it has to be remembered that the breeder has paid a stud fee, fed and housed the kittens and their dam for a considerable time—and oh, how they can eat!—and has also paid for their immunization.

It is extremely important to know where the kittens are going, for we have a great responsibility towards them. Owners can be good, bad or indifferent. The bad ones are the ones who like money better than cats, and the ones who let themselves in for more cats than they can properly look after. The person who buys a given number of Siamese cats with the idea that each queen will produce x kittens in a twelvemonth, and that each kitten can be sold for x dollars, is not truly a cat lover. He is, moreover, almost certainly doomed to disappointment. His queens will probably not present him with the desired number, or kind, of kittens. Even if they and their progeny come right up to expectations, it may prove difficult to sell the kittens: the market may be unfavourable and placing them may take a long time, during which the owner must feed and look after them. He may have to part with them at lower prices than he had hoped for. Worst of all, illness may attack his cattery, bringing vet's bills and maybe even death.

Worse, from the cats' point of view, is the owner who buys too many cats, and lets his queens have too many kittens. This is the sort of person—too often a young, silly woman—who falls in love with the Siamese kittens at a show. There is always a friend handy to say 'Oh, my dear, you must breed them! Get a really nice queen. . . .' The novice dives in enthusiastically; probably buys two queens because, the vendor tells her, 'They are so fond of each other; they may not be happy if they are separated.'. Maybe the newcomer gets a male as well: and *then*, when the kittens are paid for and in their new home, starts to enquire about breeding and feeding, and goes on quite happily for a while, maybe thinking that the prices the future kittens will fetch can pay for the food the present lot are now devouring. In a few months time, the male is living solitary in a cat-house which may or not be adequate; his few visiting queens make a lot of work, the fees they bring will not pay the expenses. Each of the two pretty little females has grown up, has a fair-sized litter, and is eagerly wolfing whatever is provided. The novice-owner does not understand that if the kittens are not fed separately, they will go hungry. She says feebly 'They look a bit thin . . . I suppose they're all right.' She does not know how to go about selling them, but cannot afford the money or the time to look after them properly. This is a disastrous home for cats.

Common, too, is the half-wit who takes home yet another kitten, seen at a show, exclaiming 'Oh! I *must* have that!' 'That' can be introduced into a pen-and-run already full of cats who were taken-a-fancy-to at some time or another; dishes of food may be set down at irregular intervals, and left, while the owner goes out for the day. The poor little new kitten will not stand an earthly chance. He will wake up every morning, young, eager, hungry . . . Nothing. In the end, he will maybe die of worms and semi-starvation, and the owner will very likely say 'I paid a lot for him—but he wasn't any good.'

The owner who is of indifferent quality is the one who has some sense but no sensibility. He may feed and house his cats quite properly, giving them adequate food, water and heating; he will not be unkind—merely unloving. In this category is the successful though not affectionate breeder. This is the one who knows exactly what is good for cats: his queens live in small compartments with small runs; here everything is clean, but nothing is 'comfy'; there is heating but no warmth, suitable food but no caresses.

The ideal owners are the people who really love their cats; who consider each one separately; who know that all cats are freedom-loving, and nearly all want to be loved. There is a judge of Siamese who said to a prospective purchaser of one of her kittens 'They live with us'. Another might have praised the looks and lineage of his wares; she boasted of their happiness, of their being, as it were, part of her family. From the cats' point of view, the perfect owner is the one who can say of his Siamese 'They live with us'.

The cats are entirely innocent and entirely dependent upon us.

We have made the struggle for survival much easier for this breed; we have provided in abundance the shelter and warmth and food which the Siamese cat asks from us, and we are giving him safety from his predators; with us he has found in plenty the things which his nature prompted him to seek, and which are giving him a fine chance in the eternal battle for the survival of the fittest; and we owe it to any kittens we breed to see that they are not sold to unsuitable homes.

### BREEDERS

South Africa is fortunate in having breeders who care for the cats and who breed to improve the type, and not for the sake of selling as many kittens as possible. Nevertheless there are here, as everywhere, people who are less worthwhile; folk who, knowing that the seal-points are still the most popular variety, breed them simply for the market, and without regard to show quality. In the Union boarding fees for cats put into kennels are not excessive. As mentioned in Chapter 5 there is a large number of boarding catteries, and it is as well to inspect them before deciding where to send a cat while, maybe, the owner goes on holiday; for as with most things, some are extremely good—and others not so very good. There are in South Africa many neutered or spayed Siamese who are the pets of their owners, and in this country of the lovely climate, they are doubtless very happy.[1]

Australia has a big and growing Siamese fancy, and so has New Zealand, whence comes, incidentally, confirmation of the undoubted fact that nature will produce, after her fashion, anything that man may claim as the result of his own experiments. I wrote, a little while ago, an article for the *Siamese News Quarterly* of America, in which was mention of one of the effects of the great popularity of Siamese: the introduction of the restrictions-of-colour-to-points coat pattern into other breeds, as Colourpoints—which started off as longhair Siamese—and Si-Rex, which are Rex (wavy-coated) cats with the restriction factor introduced; I said that obviously, for anyone who had a mind to them, Si-Manx were a possibility. '... I thought that you would be interested to hear this story of Manx-Siamese. The village of Makatu is an historic Maori settlement and . . . a holiday and sea-fishing spot. . . . One permanent resident who was away for a week or two at intervals and who left her female Manx to be fed by neighhbours invited me to call and see some unusual kittens. The kits were what you describe as "Si-Manx". At the time that I saw these "Kiwi Si-Manx" they were about eight weeks. Of an unusual dull grey colour, self-colour, that is, with black points. . . . Coat texture I can only describe as plush and semi-longhair in an even mixture. Of the two kits of the litter one was truly tailless. . . .'[2]

These kittens were not the result of one cross; a mating between a Siamese and Manx would produce kittens all carrying the gene for Siamese coat-pattern, but none showing it; a second family, with the restriction-to-points phenotype, could be achieved in several ways: the F1 kittens, mated inter se, would have a one-in-four chance of coloured points; a F1 daughter might have been mated to her Siamese sire and produced a F2 of self and Siamese patterned kits in equality; or the dam might herself have carried Siamese, in which case the pattern would appear in the F1. In all these possibilities, the arrival of two kittens both Si-Manx is not unusual, for the one-in-four or 1 : 1 ratios are the predictable results over a number of litters: the recessive restriction pattern might not appear at all in one F2 litter, whereas in another—as evidently happened—it could show in all the kittens, as it did in this instance. The Manx factor would not be a problem: Manx must now and then be crossed with tailed cats, for if they are not, disaster follows in the shape of non-viable kittens. Nature has, of course, provided for this by seeing to it that there are plenty of tailed cats on the Isle of Man. The cross with Siamese would, from the Manx point of view, be a good one, in respect of health and survival; and one 'rumpy'—a true Manx—can always be expected from a mating of rumpy to tailed cat. One interesting point about this little family is that despite the introduction of Siamese the Si-Manx kittens appear to have kept something of the very attractive double-coat for which Manx are famous. Unluckily, the Makatu Si-Manx have been lost sight of, so that their exact mode of production is not known; but they remain a good example of what can come of free matings, and of the results of letting a Siamese male roam the township!

EXPORT AND IMPORT

In Europe, kittens can quite easily be sold from one country to another; you can see the prospective purchase, his or her relatives and surroundings, just by making a journey. If you want a kitten from Britain, it is quite easy to travel across the channel and, indeed, many people go to British shows, perhaps because they have been invited to judge, maybe on a visit to their friends. The British breeder cannot easily import a cat because of his country's strong quarantine laws, but for a breeder in France to sell a kitten in Switzerland presents no difficulties. To send one further afield is not so simple.

Siamese breeders in America, South Africa or Australasia sometimes want kittens from Europe. It is not impossible to send them; the importer will want the best and will pay a high price and all the expenses, which are not inconsiderable. The exporter will, if he is wise, ask a judge of the breed to see the kitten and decide whether his show qualities are good enough, and will engage an agent to arrange all transport: an accredited agent knows all the procedure and is of enormous help. The exporter will have to provide a veterinary certificate issued within a week of shipment, which must be given in duplicate to the agent and without which the kitten would not be allowed to leave the country. He will have to send to the Governing Council Registrar, with full particulars and the appropriate fee, asking for a certified export pedigree and a certificate of transfer of ownership from himself to the purchaser; these must be forwarded to the new owner, and the kitten can travel as soon as a passage has been booked for him and the purchaser has confirmed that he will be met.

Any kitten which goes from Europe to Australia travels by air or by ship in quarantine conditions and goes into quarantine immediately on arrival; exporters say that animals shipped to Australia are beautifully cared-for. A kitten flying to America will be airborne for a few hours, and he can travel in a beautifully-constructed wooden crate of exactly the right proportions, so that he will neither be cramped nor feel himself sliding about in too big a container. These crates have room for the kitten, a folded blanket, and a very small 'scratch-tray'; they are expensive but are necessary by regulation, and well worth their price.

Breeders sending Siamese far abroad will sometimes ask—and receive—fantastic prices; in a period of rising costs it is useless to give figures; but there are one or two things to be taken into account. The purchaser will pay all expenses, from the fare and the agent's fee down to the certificates and, in many cases, the cost of vaccination and the inevitable telephone calls to vet.-surgeons, carrying agents and so on, as well as the price of the kitten. On the one hand, it is essential to send him a really fine specimen who will, barring accidents, show well, breed well, and be a credit to his breeder and his country of origin as well as being a delight to his new owner. On the other hand, breeders ought to take care to apprise themselves of the conditions their kitten will meet on arrival. It is possible for someone to buy a kitten with the sole object of winning prizes; distances between the places where shows are held are great and sometimes cats and kittens are sent from show to show, maybe in inadequate containers, just for the purpose of collecting winners' ribbons. The owner may often not travel with his exhibit, but put the matter into the hands of a carrying agent. It has even been said that such an agent may have a cat of his own to exhibit and that in this case the cat for whom his services have been hired will not show to such advantage as his own.

Even though it is the exception and not the rule for purchasers to ill-treat their animals, it is for the breeder to make absolutely sure where his kitten is going. Kittens have been sold by British breeders in Britain to the wrong kind of home; and this has happened in all countries; the breeders had not discovered what conditions would be like. How much more difficult to check on this vital point if the kitten is going many miles to a distant land.

Yet it can be done; every breeder ought to know where his kitten is going before he parts with it. In the case of the breeder who exports show-quality kittens to a far country, it would be worth while to join one of the societies or associations of that country: through this, many friends may be made, and much information obtained. In any case, whether you sell at home or abroad, for a high or for a low price, make quite sure that you are not selling your kitten 'down the river'.

If we breed for show points, and for the thrill of winning, we shall get a great deal of pleasure from the shows we attend; if we breed for money we shall not, in the long run, have much success. But if we breed for the pleasure of the company of young kittens and their mothers, if we enjoy the delight of a purchaser in his kitten even if he was not rich enough to pay a vast price, above all, if we breed for health—then we shall get all the pleasure and excitement of a delightful hobby.

We ought not to be too intense about our cats. If we take the matter of breeding and exhibiting too seriously, we shall lose the pleasure that our small Siamese friends can give us. The only things that should, in the last analysis, matter really deeply are the happiness and the well-being of the cats. Obviously a hobby is not worthwhile if it brings no excitements; but we shall spoil a pleasant game if we are too passionately anxious to win it. The modern trend is all for winning: a game, a contest of any kind—they all cause rancour because no one feels he can afford to lose. But in this matter of rearing Siamese kittens we shall lose nothing but rather gain enormously if we stick to the two essentials—the health and happiness of the breed.

Chapter seven

# Showing: I

## SHOWS IN BRITAIN

For anyone who is fond of cats, to go to a cat show is a delightful experience. Show procedure varies in different countries, but the hard work involved always brings a lot of pleasure to a lot of people. In Britain, there are shows which take place annually and which are devoted to Siamese only: those sponsored by the Siamese Cat Club, the Siamese Cat Society, the Siamese Cat Association and the Northern Siamese Cat Club. There are also plenty of classes for Siamese at the all-breed shows—the big ones such as the National and the Hertfordshire and Middlesex in London, and the not much smaller ones in the provinces, such as the Midland or the Wessex. Probably the Kensington Kitten and Neuter Cat Club's show, held in London, usually in July, is the most beautiful of them all; for apart from the neuters, all the exhibits are kittens, with the charm and sweetness that this implies.

The owner or breeder who wishes to enter his cat or kitten in a show, and who is a novice, will want information as to what shows are available for him. It is of no use to give names and addresses of secretaries, for these may change at any time for a variety of reasons; but if the novice exhibitor has joined a club, then he will be able to get all the information he needs from the club secretary; if not, there are two suggestions which may be made: first, the person who sold him his cat may be able to help; secondly, *Fur and Feather*, a fortnightly publication which is the official organ of the Governing Council of the Cat Fancy, will provide a lot of useful information. A list of shows is published in this journal at the beginning of each show season, but in any issue there are names, advertisements and letters which can help the novice (see Chapters 6 and 9).

Having found a suitable show—one which is due to take place on a convenient date and which is not so far away as to be too tiring for the exhibit—it is necessary to write to the show manager for a schedule and an entry form. The first will list what classes are available, and the second should be filled in with all possible care. A list of show rules will arrive with these papers and, if you are a novice, it is vital to read them carefully as well as to consider exactly which classes will do for your exhibit. The rules have far more importance than is generally realized by inexperienced exhibitors. For instance, one of them states that the cat to be shown must be the *bona fide* property of the exhibitor. It is fatally easy for a beginner to say 'How silly! Of course he's my property! I bought him and paid for him!' This is to think in terms of common law; to enter a cat at a show run under the rules of the Governing Council, it is necessary for him to be the property of the exhibitor *on the books of the Council.* He will have been registered with the Council by the breeder, and will appear in the Registrar's records as the breeder's property. If the breeder by any chance forgets to give the purchaser of a kitten a transfer form as well as a copy of the pedigree, then the purchaser, if he wishes to breed or to exhibit, should write and ask for the form, which requires the breeder's signature, and which explains clearly the procedure to be followed by the kitten's new owner so that the kitten shall be transferred to his name in the register.

If the rules are important, so is the schedule; many a good cat has been disqualified because his owner had not given enough thought to the matter of what classes listed in the schedule were those for which his cat was eligible. Exhibitors have sometimes, for instance, failed to notice that in a Brace class the cats are judged on their individual merit, whereas Pairs are judged by their likeness to each other. You may think that you can enter in a Pairs class two Siamese kittens of outstanding beauty; but if one is a lilac-point and the other a blue-point, they do not qualify for that particular class. The matter of the age of a kitten is also a frequent stumbling-block to new exhibitors; it is necessary to make sure your kitten will be the right age for a given class on the day of the show. Show managers are very helpful; if you send in a form with a wrong entry and the show manager notices this, he will get in touch with you and will help you to correct the matter. But sometimes the mistake is one which cannot be discovered by a show manager, such as the entry of a cat in a club class when the owner is not a member of the club concerned.

## SHOW MANAGEMENT

Very few people realise the difficulties of running a show. The show manager has to see to it that a hall is booked and the show advertised; he orders pens to be delivered and he gets the schedules printed and sent out. Then he deals with entries, sending receipts, banking the fees, getting the catalogues compiled and printed. In these days of many exhibits and growing popularity of the cats, especially Siamese, no one person could cope with all the work involved, and there is always a show committee, usually the committee of the club which is sponsoring the show. Judges have to be engaged, vet.-surgeons contacted to see if they can be in attendance, stewards arranged for, rooms booked at an hotel for judges who come from a distance; catering arrangements to be attended to at the show hall, stalls to be seen to and let for cat charities or cat accessories, lunches for the judges, safety arrangements; and always the catalogue (with the advertisements which pay for its printing), and the endless paper work and telephone calls and exhibitors wanting late entries.

A show manager and perhaps one helper may well stay up working into the small hours for days on end, dealing with correspondence and such things as judges' books, which must be done at the last minute, making sure that tallies have been sent to all exhibitors. On the night before the show he and members of his committee will be at the hall, seeing that all is in order, and examining each pen to make sure that it is safe and has proper fastenings. He must make sure that everything is ready, from the tables, bowls and disinfectant for judging to the peat-moss required for scratch-trays. It is, of course, possible for a judge to be taken ill; another will have to be found, with all that this means in the way of alterations to classes: exhibitors who are disappointed at not getting the opinion they had wished for; the possibility of finding a judge who can take some of the classes required but not all, either because he is not an all-breed judge or because he has promised them at another show in the same season. Usually a judge may not judge the same Open class twice in a season, since to become a champion a cat must win three challenge certificates at three different shows under three different judges; thus a change of judge is essential to a contender, and a judge who can help with some classes in a case of illness may not be able to help with all that are needed. The show manager will have to do quite a lot of reorganization. It is easy to replace a steward, for there are many young people who want to learn; but if a judge falls ill, the work will have to be shared out among the judges who are present. In Britain a fairly recent Governing Council Rule states that no cat or kitten may be exhibited twice within fourteen days. This is, for the cats' well-being, a splendid rule; and it has the curious effect that a judge may take the same championship classes twice in a fortnight, since the same cats cannot contend within that period.

On the day of the show, committee members will be at the entrance to the hall to sell tickets to visitors; others will see that the judges' books, tables and towels, and badges for judges and stewards are ready; yet others will sit at a table on the platform, ready to receive the award slips from the stewards, to answer queries, to deal with a hundred-and-one minutiae, such as making sure there is the proper number of catalogues set aside for judges and stewards, and attending to prize cards. The show manager will be everywhere, argus-eyed and, amazingly, always good-tempered. He is the final 'court of appeal', and often surrounded by little crowds asking questions—some of them enough to try the patience of an archangel. People who do this difficult and tiring work undertake it because they enjoy it; they are not in the ordinary sense paid: the sponsoring club votes them an honorarium, but this is a sign of appreciation, not an agreed 'rate for the job' payment. A good show manager is someone really dedicated to the work, and his reward is the success which attends his efforts. The size of shows is increasing rapidly: at the National Cat Club's very big show in London there will always be a show organizer and three show managers: for longhairs, shorthairs and Siamese. After a show, the work is not by any means finished: there is still prize-money to be sent, marked catalogues to be prepared for club secretaries, accounts to be seen to. To agree to manage a show is to undertake, from first to last, half-a-year's work.

If a show cannot be expected to be a success without an experienced show manager, it could not take place at all without the exhibits. It is not good to be slap-dash in making an entry, and this is not only to avoid giving extra work to the show manager, but because it can lead to heart-breaking disappointment. It is possible by entering your cat in a wrong class to win a championship certificate with all the delight that this will give to his proud owner—

and then to have him disqualified when it is discovered that he was not eligible for the class concerned. The instructions are clear and well-worth reading carefully, just as it is worth while to prepare your cat well for the show.

### PREPARATING FOR A SHOW

Siamese cats require daily grooming (see Chapter 5); the lovely texture of their coats is largely made up of guard-hairs, which are inclined to loosen and moult out to some degree at any time of year. The cats practically always enjoy their daily combing: they queue up to be groomed, and they enjoy having the comb run backwards through their fur, and then forward again, sleeking them down; they purr and pick up their paws and rub against their owner during this daily rite, though the kittens tend to think it a game, and to roll over, waving decidedly scratchy paws at the comb! When there is a show in view it is a good thing to follow the combing by rubbing down the beautiful coat with a chamois leather; this will produce a sheen of great beauty if it be done for several days in succession. In the case of kittens, the little fleas which appear in their fur, especially in warm conditions, are a trap for the unwary; as described in Chapter 5 a queen always kept in clean surroundings and well-groomed will very likely never have any fleas—but her kittens may! Safe insecticide powder is obtainable from reputable pet shops and from chemists, and if you intend to show a litter, it is well to watch for these little parasites in case the queen has not been able to tidy them away from her kittens' coats. They will usually appear at the lower end of the back, where the tail joins the body, and they are not exactly a disgrace: in the summertime they will be found, even in the most beautifully-run catteries, in young kittens, in old cats too tired to wash, in queens in kitten unable to wash properly. In fact it is necessary, however clean the blankets and well-scrubbed the cat-houses, to be ready to pepper the kittens with 'flea-powder' if they need it. And when it comes to showing, a flea, so plainly visible on a pale Siamese cat, would by no means impress the judge favourably!

One of the important things about showing, in fact, is that your cat should be well-presented. It is a show rule that only plain white blankets, scratch-trays and so on, may be used, and this is to ensure that there shall be no distinguishing mark. It is probable that the integrity of judges is such that none of them could be bribed or cajoled into agreeing to look for stitching on a blanket in order to give a prize to anyone's exhibit. But trouble-makers may be anywhere: if you put a green-and-red striped bowl for milk in your cat's pen, there may easily be someone to whisper 'Do you think he knows the judge?' A cat which is not competing may have a decorated pen; there are many occasions for this. There have been held exhibitions of cats where there was no competition whatever, and the people who bring their cats to such an exhibition show wonderful skill and imagination in the decoration of the pens. There was once exhibited a little Siamese female in a large pen draped with royal purple velvet, and with a small, beautifully-contrived crown on the top of the cage. Sometimes a comical slant is introduced, as when one of our very famous Siamese breeders booked a double pen for his male cat, and put the scratch-tray at one end behind a plain curtain upon which a neat lable announced 'gents'. There are often exhibition pens at the big shows, for sometimes people wish to exhibit a cat which is an example of a new variety not yet recognised and therefore not eligible for competition, thus bringing something fresh to the attention of others. But when a cat is competing it is best to keep exactly to the rules; do not leave under your pen a basket with the label and your name showing, and do not speak to the judges, even if you know them, until judging is over.

Incidentally, it is probably not necessary to leave very much in the cat's pen. Nice warm blankets, hot-water bottle in a white cover, white scratch-tray. It is a good idea to offer the cat a little of something that he fancies to eat when you first pen him: it will make him feel that this is not a bad place after all! If you offer milk or water and he does not want it, it is best to remove all feeding bowls; you will be able to go back to him and feed him as soon as the public is allowed in the hall, usually about midday; it is best to keep away from his pen if there is a judge in the vicinity.

### SETTLING IN

Upon arrival in the hall you have first to get your exhibit vetted-in. Shows are very big in these days of feline popularity: there may be thousands of exhibits at a big, all-breed show, so that although the clubs engage the services of three or four vet-surgeons, it is still necessary to wait your turn in a queue. The vets and their stewards are, however, experienced and competent, and the process of 'vetting-in' does not really take too long. A queue can be held up for a little of course if a sick cat is found. This, considering the number and size of shows, happens seldom; yet it is extraordinary that in these days of enlightenment there are still people stupid enough to bring a cat with a 'weepy' eye or even with diarrhoea to a show. Such folk are often bold enough to declare that their cat must have caught a cold on the journey.

It does not require much imagination to appreciate the disappointment of an owner who has entered a cat which seems to him to be of very high quality and finds something wrong on the eve—perhaps on the very morning—of the great day. Money has been spent, trouble taken, all arrangements made; the cat looks like a winner every time. Presumably the owner thinks that he is eating well so he can't be ill—he'll be all right when they get there. In fact, it is almost certain that the trouble will be discovered by the vet.-surgeon, and the poor cat put in an isolation pen; and the owner will suffer the humilation of seeing him—and any other exhibits that may have been brought from the same household—turned away, and of watching the vet. and his steward having a more-than-ordinarily thorough scrub with disinfectant. Rarely, an exhibit who is sick may get past the vet.-surgeon; signs of illness are not always immediately apparent. If they are discovered by a judge and his steward, the vet.-surgeon in attendance throughout the show will be asked to take a look, and if he decides that the cat is sick, this exhibit and any others from the same household will be sent away. In the meantime, irreparable damage may have been done. After one show, numerous cats were ill, and one breeder lost all her cats and kittens simply because an infected cat had been slipped in by an owner who thought that he was of championship quality, and thought of nothing else. If a cat shows the very slightest sign of ill-health it is best to keep him at home and send for his own veterinary surgeon: given ordinary luck, he will live to compete another day. However, it must be said that it is exceptional for a sick cat to get by the vets and their stewards.

### TALLIES

As a rule, before exhibitors have begun to be impatient at having to queue for veterinary attention, they will find themselves in the hall, looking for the pens alloted to them, and arranging blankets and scratch-trays prior to settling in their exhibits—round whose necks must be put the tallies with the cats' numbers, sent to the exhibitors beforehand. It is astonishing how many people, not by any means all novices, do not know how to get a tally round a cat's neck! A judge who gets through all his classes at a big show without finding at least one cat with too tightly tied a 'necklace' is lucky indeed. Cats have been seen by judges and stewards dribbling, wretched, with saliva pouring over their chests and paws, simply because a bit of elastic had been tied so tightly that they were being half-strangled.

The best way to deal with the matter of the tally is to prepare it the day before the show; use a piece of narrow white elastic, preferably not brand now, thread the tally onto it, and tie the two ends in a loose granny knot; then try the circlet on the cat. If it is too loose, tighten the knot; you can snip off the end bits if they are too long. Too loose a necklace is not good, for the cat may decide to get rid of it, and get his lower jaw under it, so that the elastic is in his mouth. But if your knot is loose when you do the 'trying on', you can tighten or loosen the elastic until it is a perfect fit. Then before putting the exhibit into his pen, you have only to slip his tally over his head. If you have more than one exhibit, it is important to put their correct tallies on each; as can be seen, to do otherwise might be to find that the judge had unwittingly awarded a prize to the less good cat or kitten. However, what is perhaps not generally realised is that, except where exhibits are sharing a pen, the importance of these tallies is not so great as might be supposed: a judge, finding a cat on the verge of strangulation, will slip off the talley as quickly as possible and ask his steward to thread it through the bars of the pen; unless there are two or more exhibits in one pen, this will be sufficient identification.

Of course, a great many exhibitors know all they need to know about putting on tallies and one exhibitor at a recent show had tied them most beautifully: the exhibits were kittens, and each wore a little collar of flat, white, silk ribbon (nothing that is not white may be used). The tallies hung from these wonderfully-contrived collars, each fitting perfectly; and each kitten had a tiny, flat bow, neat as the white tie of a pre-war dandy, tying the ribbon under his little chin. Perhaps the goddess Bast knows how such neatness was contrived!

## SHOW PRESENTATION

It is in fact very important that an exhibit should be well-presented, and this is often mentioned in judges' reports. Extreme sleekness and cleanliness both of the cat and of his appurtenances are likely to give a good impression not merely to the visiting public, but to the judge. This may sound ambiguous: a good judge, it may be thought, should be able to pick out a good cat even if he is lying on a dirty blanket; but it is not quite so simple as this. If the cat has not been properly groomed he may lose marks for 'condition' by having a rough coat, or one of those little fleas; if he is a perfectly beautiful specimen, he will get his prize even if his blankets be grubby—but how about the second and third prizes? Many a judge has had, say, an Open class for seal-pointed females; has known at once that one exhibit is outstanding and worthy of a challenge certificate; but has found it hard to decide upon the second and third prize-winners. It may be that, the winner apart, the rest of the class is rather 'so-so', with a couple of females somewhat better than the others, and of about equal merit. This is one of the difficulties constantly encountered by judges; in an effort to be perfectly fair, quite a bit of time is often spent comparing two cats of equal merit. If one is beautifully presented and the other looks 'messy', then this may be the deciding factor.

Extraordinary as it may seem, there are some exhibits who refuse to be well-presented! Sometimes they are litters of kittens who throw everything in sight about, making an untidy playroom of their double pen. But often they are grown cats—sometimes feeling bad-tempered, but occasionally just simply 'ornery'. A well-arranged pen occupied by a tearaway can become like a gipsy encampment in a matter of minutes! The cat will scrabble his blankets into an untidy heap, and often tear into strips the clean white paper on the floor of his pen; he will upset a bowl of water if the owner has mistakenly left one for him; he will kick the contents of his scratch-tray sky-high—and the creamy coat of a Siamese stuck full of peat-moss looks like something from the outer space of science fiction. And all this not necessarily in temper or in play, but 'just for kicks'. The owner, if he is watching the judging from the gallery must, on seeing the judge and steward trying to disentangle all this, feel very badly let-down by his cherished little friend with the blue eyes!

There are, however, worse hazards than untidiness. With all the care that is taken, it is still possible for a cat to escape. This does not often happen, for everyone connected with cat shows knows that constant vigilance is the price of safety; but sometimes a voice on the loud-hailer will say 'close all doors!' and this means that a cat or kitten is free in the hall. I cannot recall an instance of a cat who escaped during a show and was not recaptured; there are, indeed, few such escapes. There were two Siamese kittens, some few years ago, who were apparently completely lost, and occasioned great anxiety until they were discovered in the car park, sitting peacefully on the roof of their own car! There was a young Siamese queen quite recently who got out from the very back of her pen, where a couple of wires were loose, and where no one would think of checking since the wiring was against a metal sheet. A visitor to the show tapped me on the shoulder and, without uttering a sound, pointed: and there was her little majesty sitting on top of the pen quite calmly surveying her surroundings! I took three strides, stepping softly, and firmly seized her; she was quite happy to sit in my arms until a safe pen was arranged for her. Yet if there had been no sharp-eyed, quiet bystander, and no one to take her quietly and without fuss, she could have taken fright and been lost to view, maybe under a pile of stacked chairs, terrified of pursuers and determined not to be caught.

### SHOW TEMPERAMENT

Fear is, usually, the cause of bad behaviour in these cats. One of our senior judges, than whom there is no better judge of Siamese, was attacked by a cat who had been placed on the table in front of her to be considered for a best-in-show award. She was severely bitten and scratched, and must have suffered very great pain—but she did not let the cat go. He, excusably if unfortunately, had been frightened—by the crowds, the loud-speaker, flashlight pictures being taken, the general brouhaha of the show. Sometimes male cats will become angry with their neighbours; a couple of males disliking the scent of each other can cause a lot of trouble. The most frequent cause is the presence of a calling queen. It is a mistake to bring a female in season to a show (see p. 160) but it is fair to say that in the case of a queen just beginning to call, the owner may not know that she is in season. The males in the opposite pens, however, will be fully aware of the situation. Some cats are so sweet-tempered with humans that they can be judged even if they have a quarrel with the boy next door; but others, in a fury of exasperation, would bite anything that came in their way, including the steward's hand; such cats are not able to be handled and must perforce be disqualified. Some cats are inclined to become a trifle jumpy and ill-tempered towards the end of a show; they have been handled by several judges, spent a long time away from their own familiar surroundings, and been shut up for hours in a confined space, all of which can try their patience.

There are, however, some—and many of them are Siamese—who are born show cats: it is plain to see that such a cat is pleased to be at the show, delighted with the crowds, and glorying in the admiration which he receives. You can see a cat of this disposition walking close to the front of his pen, rubbing against the bars, looking with pleased eyes at his admirers—in fact, doing all he can to invite the plaudits of his audience! He will purr appreciation if he be touched, and it is very important that none but the owner and the officials shall touch an exhibit: just in case there should be an undesirable germ on an apparently healthy little nose, it is far best not to risk carrying it on a fingertip to another exhibit.

Visitors to cat shows see the cream of the fancy, and a great many people come to these shows. Besides not touching the exhibits for fear of infection, the visitor should remember that sudden noise frightens cats. Often people bring small children with them, and many children are born cat lovers: very young people indeed have acted as second steward to a judge and been of great help. But I have seen a kitten severely scratch two judges and a steward before he was put back in his pen simply because a small boy blew a whistle almost in his face as he was being judged. You could not expect a little boy to know that if you have a nice whistle it had better not, in some circumstances, be used—but it would be good if the grown-ups told the children that a sudden noise may terrify a cat or kitten. Again, it is very unkind both to the cats and to the judges to take a flash picture while the exhibits are being judged for best-in-show awards. The cat is on the table, being quietly passed along the line of judges, with a steward waiting at the end of the table with his basket; there is a sudden flash in the cat's face and, terri-

programmes, without having the faintest idea what are their politics, how much they pay the income tax man, nor whether their home lives are satisfactory; you all share a love for Siamese cats, and this brings the friendship of those who are united in a common interest. Thus the newcomer to the Siamese fancy will easily make friends and gain information in discussions with other exhibitors.

There are always prizes to be won: even at a small exemption show, where no challenge certificates may be awarded and where the rules, though conforming with those of the Governing Council, are much less stringent, awards are made to the winners. A sanction show is a rehearsal for a championship show: the Council will grant permission for a championship show to a club or society which has run one or more very good sanction shows. At all these there will be first, second, third and reserve prizes, with their red, blue and white cards, and also VHC, HC and C cards (very highly commended, highly commended and commended), which carry no money prizes as do first second, third and reserve, but which are nevertheless worth having: They signify that the judge has thought too well of the exhibit to pass him over. In an unusually good class, a card of commendation may easily be awarded to a cat who would have been among the first three in less magnificent company.

### CHALLENGE CERTIFICATES AND BEST-IN-SHOW AWARDS

At the championship shows are awarded the coveted challenge certificates; these are for adult cats in their open classes, and three must be won under three different judges at three different shows before the cat can become a champion or, in the case of a neuter, a premier. The Governing Council sends medals to the new champions and premiers when particulars are sent to its secretary. A challenge certificate is worth having, for it will not be awarded if the judge considers that the best exhibit in the class is not worthy of it. Disappointing though it must be to find that your cat is '1st; challenge certificate withheld', it does make those certificates which are awarded really worth the winning. At some shows judges are asked to nominate their Best-of-Breed in open classes, and these may be judged against each other for Best-in-Show awards by a panel of judges, going to the pens, thus avoiding the sometimes difficult business of taking the exhibits to the platform.

fied, he bites and claws whatever is near him—the judge's hands—and bites the harder if the necessary restraint is put upon him to prevent escape. A lot of harm can be done before he is safe back in his basket—and it is not the cat's fault.

As against the cat who thoroughly enjoys every minute of a show and the cats who are happy enough until they become tired is the little cat who is terrified of show surroundings and conditions and whom nothing can sooth. Such a cat ought not to be shown a second time; it is heartbreaking to own a Siamese potential champion and to find that his terror of shows is so great that it is cruel to exhibit him, and that he will never get more than one challenge certificate. But this is not really a very common situation, and the great majority of owners can settle their exhibits into the pens and, having made sure the bars and the fastenings are safe (the show manager will always have strong wire in reserve), can prepare to enjoy the day.

### THE EXCITEMENT OF THE SHOW

Only judges and stewards are allowed in the aisles when judging starts; exhibitors can watch the judging from a gallery, and at a given time—nearly always midday—the public is admitted. There is an exhilaration about a cat show for those fond of these creatures: the beautiful exhibits in their pens, the judges and stewards in white overalls, the stalls, with gay kitten toys and feline accessories such as baskets, bowls and travelling hampers; the table on the platform with the show manager and his helpers, and below the dais a row of special pens where the best-in-show exhibits will be placed—all this creates a pleasurable excitement for those participating. Novices are not the only exhibitors by any means; anyone visiting a show will find the Siamese penned in one section of the hall, and the catalogue will tell him what cats are present, by whom bred and who are the owners. Many of these breeders and owners have been fanciers for years, and will be happy to talk about their experiences to any 'new boy' (or girl) whom they may meet. There is always a sense of camaraderie among people with the same interests: if you are devoted to Siamese, and you go to a Siamese show, or to that section of an all-breed show reserved for Siamese, you will be surrounded by people who share your love for these cats. It is possible to work with people for years, on committees, at shows, in breeding

Besides these awards, there will be special prizes, offered by clubs, by manufacturing firms or by individuals: these will be for winners of certain classes, or for particular characteristics, as 'for the cat over two years with the deepest eyecolour'. These prizes may be in cash or kind, or they may be the trophies of the club which offers them: in the latter case there may be added to the offer 'must have been bred by exhibitor. Five wins.' This virtually ensures that the trophy concerned remains the club's property for ever; but trophies which require only three wins have often been won outright by some outstanding cat; the proud owner very often replaces the cup he has won by giving a new trophy to the club. Many clubs will allow winners to take a trophy to be held for one year; and many give commemorative shields or rosettes for wins.

In addition to these awards there are the best-in-show rosettes to be won. As the show proceeds, award cards are put on the pens, red, blue and yellow, as a rule, for first, second and third, white for reserve and for VHC, HC or C. The Stewards will have taken the award slips to the table as each class is judged, and these will in due course be affixed to an award-board, where exhibitors may see them. The judges will also send up to the table their nominations for best-in-show and, in the afternoon, panels of judges, usually five in number, will be called upon in turn to take their places on the platform. The first panel will decide which are the best longhair adult, kitten and neuter and which of these is the best longhair exhibit in the show; the second panel will decide upon the shorthairs in the same manner, and finally a third assesses the Siamese.

The exhibits nominated by the various judges are brought to the platform in their own baskets by the stewards, and are passed down the line of judges, who have each a towel, a bowl of disinfectant water and a pad of paper on the table in front of them. The judges do not discuss the exhibits, but write down their numbers and wash their hands after handling each, as they did when judging their various classes, and then put the number of the cat of their choice on a folded paper, so that this is a ballot for best-in-show. The show manager and one of his helpers then look at the papers and the name of the winner is announced. The exhibits chosen are held up by the stewards to receive their round of applause, and they are then placed in the pens below the dais, each with a big commemorative rosette, and the visitors to the show can see the cream of the fancy displayed at their very best. To be best Siamese at any championship show may well make the owner and breeder proud, for these cats have been bred to perfection, and competition is very keen.

Chapter eight

# Showing: II

### SHOWS IN THE USA

In America, there are comparatively few clubs catering for Siamese only (as fully discussed in Chapter 9). However, many cat shows take place throughout the length and breadth of the country, and quite a few are specialty shows, or have specialty rings at all-breed shows; so that Siamese are well represented at the big exhibitions. You may have a six-ring show, each ring conducted by a different judge, and there may be more than one ring in which a Siamese may be entered.

Cats are never carried to the judging ring in baskets, the reason being that it is considered that anyone seeing a cat in a basket will conclude that he is difficult to handle. It is well known that a cat confined for a day—and sometimes for two days—in a small space, surrounded with strangers, handled by people he does not know and, in fact, not able to live in his accustomed manner, may at last take fright, try frantically to escape, and scratch or bite the person who endeavours to stop him. Naturally, no two cats are alike: there are many so gentle they are never difficult to handle; some are calm, some are regular little 'show-offs'; some are too nervous to be fit to show, and a few will take an exhibition sweetly until at last something alarms them, and they become crazy with fright. There is a school of thought which considers that *all* cats should be carried in baskets to the ring; this would protect them from the sights and sounds of big crowds, and would be fair-for-all. No one would be able to say that such-and-such a cat was put in a basket because he was dangerous to handle. In Britain it is common practice for stewards to take the cats in their baskets to the platform for best-in-show judging; if there should be a nervous cat who will not be handled, he will be put straight back in his own hamper, and no criticism can be levelled at the better-behaved exhibits, since they have all arrived at the judges' table in their own containers.

## AMERICAN SHOW RULES

American show rules look more complicated than they really are. The nine organizations concerned (see Chapter 3) have not long since revised these rules: Cat Fanciers Federation and American Cat Federation in 1977, for instance. These are issued in large, wonderfully-edited magazine-style brochures, and they all appear to be at one on fundamental issues such as veterinary matters, though some will stress one point, and some another. Occasionally a directive will be included which is peculiar to one particular organization; an example is CFF's rule governing the costume and behaviour of its judges. This section is headed *show decorum*: 'Judges must present a neat, *conservative* appearance in the ring, with *appropriate* dress . . . A judge will wear no jewelry which could scratch . . . a cat. A judge will drink no intoxicating beverages while in the judging ring; suspicion of intoxication . . . will result in immediate suspension.' A judge may not so much as take a glass of wine at luncheon, and it is stated that 'They must not be under the influence of drugs.'

The best instructions in this section concern smoking, which is not permitted for the judge except during intervals, and the statement 'a judge should lift a cat by supporting it from beneath, never lifting it by the neck'. In fact, it would be best for the exhibits if smoking were forbidden in all show halls; people could always enjoy a cigarette or a pipe in one of the restaurants or lounges, and the cats would be the better for a nicotine-free atmosphere. As for the instruction not to lift a cat by the scruff, it may be thought superfluous, for most people know that it is not at all good for a cat to be picked up in this way; but American judges are much younger than most judges in Europe: quite young people may have learnt precisely how to judge a cat, and yet may require to be told such things as this; especially since a judge in his twenties will not have had experience as a steward; for in America there are no stewards to take the cat onto the table for the judges' inspection. Apprentice judges will have had a good deal of experience but will not have handled so many exhibits as do the stewards in other countries. There is a judging ring, with one judge who conducts the whole show. Fewer Siamese were shown in 1976–77 than in former years, an average at any given show being 16 adult Siamese; however, it must be remembered that red-, cream-, tortie- and tabby-pointeds are recognized by seven governing bodies, while CFA and ACA do not recognize these as Siamese, but designate them 'colourpoints'. The exhibits are penned by their owners in cages behind the judge's table, and the judge will himself take the cats in turn from their pens, examine them, and put them back; he will scrub down the table as well as washing his hands after each cat that he handles. He will be attended by a clerk, who marks results from the judging slips, deals with queries and the like; no one, until he is himself a judge, has the opportunity to handle the cats in the ring.

The exhibitors sit opposite the judge's table, and if an exhibit should prove unmanageable, a clerk may, at the judge's request, ask the owner to handle it. The number of exhibits is much smaller than in Britain, where at the Siamese Cat Association's show (for Siamese only) in 1969, there were more than 300 cats and kittens, and at a big all-breed show such as the National, 400 out of 15,000 exhibits were Siamese. However, there is in America a very large number of shows. The show season starts anew each Mayday: during the 1976–77 season, 345 shows were promoted with a total of 81,310 entries. The 'gate' is very big; visitors to a show in America may number anything from 2,000 to 9,000.

A kitten may not be shown in America at less than four months, and a cat is deemed to be adult at eight months. In Europe, he remains, for show purposes, a kitten until he is nine months old. As in the rules of the Governing Council of the Cat Fancy, so in those of ACA, no declawed cat may be shown. In the Crown Cat Fanciers Federation's rules, section 7, subsection F, 'Any cat that has been declawed will not be penalized therefore'; but in the CFA rules, 'A cat not having its claws may not receive any award in a championship or premiership class' (see Chapter 5). Judges are paid. There is a definite rate-for-the-job which varies from one governing body to another: the Cat Fanciers Association pays a colour or breed specialty judge a per capita fee of 50 cents per cat, 75 cents per cat for All-Breed judges. CFA allows its clubs to accept 175 entries for one-day shows and 350 entries for two-day shows.

There are four championship classes: *Novice* for cats eight months or over who have not won a winners ribbon; *Open* for those who have not completed requirements for championship; *Champion* for cats who have won four winners ribbons; and *Grand Champion* for cats who have completed grand championships. The

Premiership classes are listed in the same manner, and ribbons are blue, red and yellow for first, second and third. If any exhibit scores a win putting him into a higher class at one show after he was entered for another show he can be transferred to the new class by the entry clerk on arrival at the later show.

## JUDGES AND SHOWS IN EUROPE

Rules for the appointment of judges are very strict in Europe. In Britain, Siamese judges are at present appointed by a panel of senior judges which, in turn, is elected by an advisory committee consisting of two delegates from each of the Siamese clubs. Anyone may apply to be considered as a judge provided he has stewarded twelve times for at least six different judges; he will be interviewed by the panel and may apply again if he is not successful. Clubs concerned with other breeds appoint their judges by committee decision : a committee, consisting probably largely of judges of the breed in question, may be expected to have observed the ability of members as stewards, breeders and exhibitors. Over many years I cannot recall any case of error in electing a judge. The acid test is always the decision of the exhibitors and show managers; mistakes on the part of a judge would mean indignation among the former and a decision by the latter never again to engage that particular judge. Indeed, it has been said that 'a bad judge would only judge once'. All appointments in Britain must be ratified by the Governing Council, and a successful applicant for appointment as a judge of Siamese will be a probationer judge at first, not entitled to judge Open Adult classes, but entitled to judge kittens, and side classes.

Under FIFE, (see Chapter 9), a would-be judge must have stewarded at four international shows, and have acted as pupil-judge at six such shows; after this, he may take a written and oral examination before two existing judges, these latter to have judged for at least five years at international shows. An international show must consist of at least 100 exhibits. The examinations are to be either for shorthairs or for longhairs; both may be taken, so that it is possible for a candidate to become an all-breed judge; but both may never be sat for at the same time. If a longhair judge wants to become a judge of shorthairs also, he must go through the same programme as before as steward and pupil-judge. A pupil-judge is asked to officiate at one or two shows in countries other than his own, and he must be able to speak at least two languages. Shorthairs, with reference to judging qualifications in Europe, include Siamese. Breeders on the continent of Europe have the great advantage of being able to breed, exhibit and sell cats internationally with no particular difficulty. I recently saw a very good seal-pointed male at a show in Rotterdam, whose breeder was French and whose owner lives in Switzerland. With no quarantine restrictions and no real travel difficulties, the Siamese fancier in Europe has a good choice of studs, of kittens to buy and markets for his own kittens, and of excellently-run shows where he can exhibit or can see the exhibits of other fanciers.

Shows on the continent are big with, usually, a preponderance of Siamese. With a few exceptions, notably in Paris, where at some shows the exhibits are judged before their pens as in Britain, the judging takes place in a ring, with a table for the judge, and the cats are brought to the table by the stewards. There are empty pens in the judging ring, so that the judge or judges can ask the stewards to pen their exhibits for comparison: often two judges will confer together as to which male, female, kitten or neuter is to have the best-in-show award. These big, international exhibitions are frequently two-or even three-day shows, and this must be tiring for the exhibits, who may, however, sometimes be taken away for the night and brought back to the show hall in the morning. A cat already a champion may compete for an international championship, for which he must win three certificates awarded by three different judges in two different countries. These international champions may compete against each other in champion of champion classes—for males or females—where the winner gets the honour and glory but no further title.

The vase of Sèvres porcelain offered by the President of the Republic for the best group of cats all bred by the same breeder has been awarded several times to Siamese. M. Mordasini of Geneva received this award for his International Champion, Mali de Surabaya, a beautiful seal-point male to whom I remember awarding a challenge certificate at Rotterdam. M. Mordasini had bought this cat from a member of the Association Féline de France, Mme Cellier Abry, who won the President's Trophy two years in succession, first with Int: Ch: Katia de Surabaya and Int. Ch. Mali, seal-points, and Ch. Opale de Surabaya and Ch. Nausicaa de Surabaya, blue-points; and then with the same group less Mali, who had gone to his new owner. This vase has also been won by Mme Desramaut with Reginald de Gravenoire, blue-point, and four young cats sired by him.

## BELGIUM AND THE NETHERLANDS

In Belgium, medals for the best cats are offered at the important shows: one is offered by the Sovereign at Antwerp; this club became the Royal Cat Club of Antwerp under King Leopold. I have seen one of these medals, won in 1965; it is a beautiful award, inscribed 'Don de S. M. le roi Baudouin. Société Royale des Amis du Chat', and it was awarded for 'The presentation quality of chestnut browns'. Not all Siamese lovers will be acquainted with chestnut browns, although they are descended from a seal-pointed Siamese male called Tombee, who belonged to Miss Wells, and who carried the gene for chocolate (brown). These cats, at their best, have coats the colour of a bright, polished 'conker' (horse-chestnut), and their eyes are lime-green. The first of them was bred in Britain in the country near Reading by the late Mrs Monro-Smith: his dam was a black shorthair carrying the factor for brown and Tombee, a good, strong, Siamese male, was his sire. This kitten was called Elmtower Bronze Idol, and became a famous cat. Unluckily, chestnut browns, sometimes called Havana browns, have appeared in Britain with colouring rather dull, as though there was unnecessary blue in their ancestry; but in the Netherlands they have the original shining coats and lime-green eyes of their Siamese-bred ancestor of years ago. The best shorthair at Eindhoven in 1969 was one of these cats, the decision being made by two English judges, Mrs Thake and myself; and the Sovereign's medal that I saw was won by the cats of very well-known breeders, Ir en Mevrouw Damsteeg. I saw also a medal, won at Antwerp, which was presented by the Governor of the Province of Antwerp at the exhibition of De Vrienden der Kat in 1964; and yet another is offered by the Municipality of Antwerp.

In Holland also, medals are presented: once a year at Amsterdam, which has the biggest show in Europe, from the Sovereign; and at Rotterdam, the Lord Mayor offers a silver medal for the best-cared-for household pet cat. These trophies are well-worth competing for. Before the second world war, such medals were offered for longhairs only. However, in 1957, at a show given by the Royal Cat Club de Belgique, a seal-pointed Siamese male, Champion Lancy King Khan, imported from Britain, was best cat in show, and won the medal offered by HM King Baudouin. In the following year, Silver Star, seal-pointed son of King Khan who was by then an international champion, was best shorthair in the Netherlands, and was awarded the silver medal offered by HRH Prince Bernhard of the Netherlands.

Medals have been offered by persons of importance in Belgium for blue-pointed Siamese, and one of these was won by a cat shown by Dr Mignon of France. I have seen a medal offered by HM King Baudouin for a group of 'best exhibits' shown by the same owner-breeder, and which was won by Ir en Mevrouw Damsteeg: their winning exhibits were chestnut browns, Abyssinians, Manx and—a lilac-pointed Siamese, Edwardian Aspen, imported from Britain.

All the shows in Holland are very effectively organized, and for admirers of Siamese it is interesting to see the many exhibits which are brought from other countries, and to compare them.

### CANADA

There are some extremely beautiful Siamese cats in Canada, and three major associations to care for them and other cats; one, the Canadian Cat Association, is a partner in the American ICA (Independent Cat Associations) group, which includes CCA as well as all the American governing bodies except CFA. Plainly, ICA makes for unity, and this is a good thing; but it would be a mistake to do away altogether with independence, and a very bad thing to have the whole cat fancy, let alone the entire Siamese fancy, cut to pattern. It has seriously been suggested that with proper, scientific breeding, cats conforming precisely to the standard could and should consistently be bred. Any child could see that if this be true and be put into effect, the pleasure of cat shows would be a thing of the past, since all the cats would, according to the standard for their variety, be exactly alike. Such a degree of equality not only could not occur but would be undesirable if it could! Agreement as to procedure in the Siamese fancy is, however, in every way desirable; like rules and like standards used throughout a continent are of value to the whole business of breeding and exhibiting. Indeed, one breeder has made the journey from Toronto to Florida with her queen so as to take her to the stud she most admired. Such interchanges are good and, between America and Canada, there is also exchange of judges. It is even hoped that there will eventually be a single registry, which would certainly greatly simplify the work of future historians of the cat fancy.

Interesting points are raised by some of the rules of the Canadian Cat Association. One of these, which comes under the heading 'Duties of Show Officials' runs: 'The show committee shall ensure that adequate lighting is provided in the judging area, so that judges may clearly distinguish the exact shade of eye and coat colour of each entry.' Good lighting is extremely important to the appraisal of a Siamese; it is, for instance, very difficult indeed to judge the points-colour of the lilac-pointeds if the light is not good. A great difficulty arises when, as happens in some of the halls engaged for shows, there is a mixture of daylight and artificial lighting. The best lighting I have seen was in the Phillips Jubilee Hall at Eindhoven, where the artificial daylight was perfection. This CCA rule is surely one which any judge of Siamese would applaud.

The next section of the same article of the CCA rules has 'A minimum of eight judging cages must be provided in each ring, with greater numbers preferred, particularly for shows with over 150 entries. Stacking of cages will not be permitted and judging cages must be separated by sheets of heavy cardboard or similar material.' This again is an admirable rule for all cats, not least for Siamese. It would be very bad to stack the cages, just as an adequate number of pens is essential for a judging area; and anyone confronted by a class of Siamese males will agree with the idea of well-separating the pens with heavy material. For as already mentioned, a whole male may become aware that somewhere in the show hall there is a little charmer about to start calling; if he decides to 'spray' his surroundings in consequence, the fury of the boy penned next to him will know no bounds, and one or both may become impossible to handle. This is one reason why calling queens are not permitted to be shown; but an owner may be caught unawares. The little madam may leave home like a big kitten and arrive at the show hall a grown-up young queen; and nice, gentle Siamese males will, in the face of this situation and enclosed in pens, hate each other very much, and be ready to tear anything apart in sheer frustration.

No judge at a show run under CCA rules may be asked to handle more than 150 cats in one day, and he will be paid a fee of $35-50 for a one-day show and $50-80 for a two-day show, plus all expenses. 'Whenever possible they are to judge the lighter colour classes prior to those of the darker shades, i.e., lilac-point Siamese through chocolate, blue, to seal-points.' The reason for this rule is not clear, but it seems that it may be simply a decision to fall into line with the United States where this procedure is followed. Whereas in America judges clean tables for themselves after each exhibit, the CCA has under 'Duties of Show Officials', section 9, 'The show management shall provide a strong adequate table or bench as the judge's working area, covered in a washable material such as heavy plastic, sponges, paper towels, disinfectants and containers shall be provided for the judge and stewards appointed to clean cages in each ring.' In Canada, exhibitors may display ribbons won by an exhibit at other shows on the inside of the cage at the back. (This is not the pen from which the cat will be judged: he will be taken from his exhibition pen to the judging area when his turn comes). A cattery name, also, may be displayed for advertising purposes, but it is the public who see these, not the judge. The show rules include a list of breeds whose champions may compete for grand championships: a winner will receive one point for every champion he defeats in his class. In these rules, Siamese come at the bottom of the shorthair list, but only because it is put in alphabetical order. Canada has her share of beautiful Siamese, and the breed is as well-loved here as elsewhere.

### SOUTH AFRICA

In South Africa also, these cats are well-loved: 'As is normal all over the world, Siamese are by far the most popular and numerous of pedigree cats in this country, and the bulk of show entries is made up by the various coloured Siamese.'[1] The cat fancy in South Africa is comparatively young: here the first show took place in 1949 and now, 30 years later, there are still only five cat clubs; all five are all-breed clubs, but in each Siamese breeders form the majority of members. At the early shows 70-80 entries could be expected; but nowadays there are more shows and the number of entries will be very much larger, with Siamese making up the biggest classes. The Johannesburg and Capetown shows, the biggest in the Union, usually have up to 200 pedigree cats and 20-30 household pets; this is a bigger entry than is usually found for one show in America where, however, there are incomparably more shows. It has to be remembered that the white population of South Africa is not enormous, so that there are necessarily fewer breeders of cats in general and Siamese in particular than in some countries; but interest in the South African cat fancy is growing and some of the new Siamese colours—tortie-points, tabby-points and red-points—are to be seen in the show pens; a tabby-tortie-point was, in fact, imported into South Africa from Britain in 1968. The seal-points are, as they always have been, the most popular Siamese, with blue-points running them a close second and lilac-points much favoured; these colours are more popular than are the new varieties. This is not surprising, and it is likely that the same situation still exists in Britain. A curious fact is that the chocolate-points of South Africa are few, and are seldom of good type; this is odd because recent chocolate-points in Britain are of truly outstanding quality, whereas informed opinion in the South African fancy is that Siamese of colours other than chocolate are of at least as good if not of better quality than those to be seen in Britain.

There are not many shows—perhaps six championship events a year. Because of the distances to be travelled, a custom prevails which was common in the very early days in Britain: cats are sent from afar and met, no longer at the railway station but at the airport, by the show manager, who attends to the boarding, vetting-in and penning of these visitors, and sees them safely off on their return journeys after the show. Many people, however, bring their own exhibits for long journeys, and some use caravans for themselves and their cats.

The British standards are used in South Africa, and shows are run in much the same manner as in Britain. In the Union it is thought that to judge the cats at their pens is preferable to the European and American practice of carrying them across the hall in the arms of stewards or clerk, for fear of the sudden, flying leap that could lose an exhibit. Indeed, when a cat has to be carried, it is best, however placid he seems, to hold him firmly and to be ready to tighten one's grip at any second.

In South Africa judging starts at 8.30 a.m. (an hour-and-a-half earlier than in Britain) and is completed by 1.00 p.m. The ideal climate of this country is a godsend to the cats and their breeders, for the kittens and their dams can be out-of-doors practically all the year round, and the question of artificial heating hardly ever arises (although, even in colder latitudes Siamese can go out in almost any weather and, much as they enjoy central heating, a prolonged hot-house atmosphere is not really good for them). The South African fancier, however, knows that his cats will never lack fresh air and sunshine. There is strict training for would-be judges, and it is a long training, comprising lectures and a good deal of study, at the end of which come oral, written and practical tests.

### SPECIAL PRIZES

In South Africa, as in Britain, cats already champions may compete for best-in-show awards, though there are in the union, as in America, grand championships to be won. The word 'special' as used in the Anglo-Saxon countries' respective cat fancies can be misleading. In Britain 'a special' is a shortened form of 'a special prize'. These prizes are always listed at the backs of catalogues, and they may be offered by almost anyone for practically any quality; club secretaries are charged with the work of offering on behalf of their clubs, at whatever shows may be designated by their committees, cups and trophies which have been given by members to the clubs; conditions for wins are usually hard, and it is generally required that they be won three or perhaps five times at different shows, in different years, by the same or by different cats according to the wishes of the giver. These are often commemorative trophies, with the name of a loved and departed cat engraved upon them; and some small token, a teaspoon, a certificate, a rosette or shield, will be given by the club, or by the donor's arrangement, to the winners; and the requirements for a win range from, say, 'best blue-pointed adult in show' to 'the seal-point with the best eye-shape' or 'the cat with the sweetest disposition'. Some clubs arrange for winners to hold for one year trophies won by their exhibits. Sometimes special prizes are offered by firms of manufacturers of feline foods or accessories, and sometimes by individuals. It is not unknown for a judge, confronted with a very good class but only a limited number of awards to bestow, to ask the show committee to accept a small special prize for a beautiful cat so unlucky as to be in a class with even more handsome exhibits. But always, in Britain, such extra awards, from the most valuable antique silver trophy to £1 offered by an individual, are referred to colloquially as 'specials'. In America, the word 'specialty' (not speciality) is used to designate a one-breed show, as for Siamese only, and in South Africa 'specials' are what in Britain are known as best-in-show awards. The Society rosettes for Best Adult, Best Kitten and Best Neuter of the Siamese Cat Society of America may be bought and offered at any show for a nominal sum, and are very handsome.

### JUDGING

Judging for these awards is carried out in the Union as on the continent of Europe, not as in Britain. British show managers arrange for a panel of judges to officiate for each breed present; usually, at an all-breed show, there will be a panel of five for long-hairs, a similar one for shorthairs and yet another for Siamese. The breeds are judged in that order and the panels, always consisting of judges of the breeds concerned, sit on a dais at a long table furnished with bowls of disinfectant-and-water, towels, and pads of writing-paper; the exhibits, which are the cats and kittens who have won in their respective classes competing against each other, are brought to the platform in their own baskets by stewards, and passed along the table to be inspected by the members of the panel, who give their verdict by ballot and without discussing the exhibits with each other. Results are announced through loud-speaker by the show manager; judging is for best male, best female, best kitten, best neuter and finally best exhibit in show. The winning cats or kittens are held up by stewards for the public to see. In the case of Siamese there could be five exhibits competing against each other: a seal-point, a blue-point, a chocolate-point, a lilac-point and a tabby-point; if the members of the panel should each cast their vote for a different exhibit, the referee judge would give the final verdict. In South Africa, however, as in Europe, judges confer together to arrive at a decision as to best-in-show exhibits. The cats selected by the judges are placed by stewards in pens in the judging area, and the judges can inspect them quietly and agree among themselves as to which is best. It is not always easy to arrive at a decision, for these exhibits are the best of the fancy, and are likely all to be of great merit, but it usually does not take long for senior judges to decide the awards. Indeed, there was an instance in Europe of two Siamese judges called upon to decide which were best male, best female, best kitten and best neuter from eight exhibits; each judge had nominated the best in her classes, so that four of the eight cats had been 'sent up for best in show' by one judge and four by the other. One said that she preferred her own male exhibit, but thought the other judge's female the better; judge no. 2 agreed, and added that her own kitten nomination was the better, but her neuter less good than his opposite number. 'I think so, too,' said judge no. 1, and the whole discussion had taken only a few moments. One of the exhibitors asked unhappily how such momentous decisions could be made so quickly—but this was, in fact, good judging: if there had been hesitation and argument, then one judge must have been wrong.

Exhibitors are entitled to watch judging, and they may not always approve of what they see. At a show in England some few years ago, one judge had a class where the exhibits, quite numerous, faced each other across an aisle. The three cats who were, in the judge's opinion, best in the class all happened to be penned on the same side of the aisle; it was said by an exhibitor that no proper attention had been paid to the occupants of the opposite pens. In fact, the steward concerned would have seen to it that his judge handled every cat. Though the odds against such an occurrence must be longish, in a fairly large Siamese class the three cats numerically first, second and third have at least once been judged best second-best and third-best in the same order.

Stewards have a good deal of responsibility. Not only must they make sure that their judges do not cross-judge—that is, do not place a cat above another in one class and below in a second class; they also risk being scratched or bitten if anything should frighten an exhibit, and they have the work of seeing that the right cats go to the dais at the right time for best-in-show judging. There are some people who make extraordinarily good stewards, and who do not themselves ever want to become judges; indeed, it has been said that it is better to be a steward, for so many unkind remarks are made about judges! No praise is too high for a really good steward.

In South Africa, show managers are dedicated cat-lovers and are not paid. In most of the Anglo-Saxon speaking countries, insurance is taken out, by rule, to cover possible losses or disasters at shows; but in South Africa judges are not paid any fee but only as in Britain, their expenses. The South African judges and stewards, of whom there are usually two or three for each judge, have always had trolley tables. In Britain, until only a few years ago, quite heavy tables had to be carried to the pens; this was difficult, especially in the big, mixed classes, where the contenders could be in various parts of a large hall, and particularly so in the afternoon, when the aisles were packed with visitors to the show. It was one of our best-known judges and Show-Managers, Mr John Shewbridge of the Bedford Cat Club, who made the prototype of the excellent trolley tables now used at all British shows. It should be noted that, with regard to size, shows can reach saturation point: the number of entries is limited by the size of the hall, so that frequently promoters of an exhibition will, in the schedule, set a limit to the number of entries that can be accepted. Thus in many cases shows are no bigger than they were some years ago; the number of Siamese entered, however, remains high.

Chapter nine

# Clubs, associations and registration

The Siamese Cat Club is the biggest specialist cat club in the world; and in Britain alone there are 12 clubs and societies devoted to the interests of this one breed. In other countries all over the world there are associations formed to cater for these cats and their owners, and also many all-breed clubs which include in their membership owners of Siamese.

The work done by the clubs is not always understood by fanciers. The bigger associations run annual shows, championship shows, maybe in London or New York or in Johannesburg, so that the members and other fanciers can see what work is being done, and what money is being spent: they can observe that a hall has been engaged and a lot of work done to provide an interesting exhibition at which members' cats as well as those of other people can be entered and may win prizes. But it is not always realised what work is done by the smaller clubs which do not run shows; people wonder how the annual subscriptions are used, and what is done for the members and their cats.

## CLUB COMMITTEES

To understand the usefulness of a cat club it is necessary to look into the work done by its committee. The matter of money is, of course, plainly set out in the balance sheet, available to all members at the time of the annual general meeting; most clubs send out their statement of accounts, duly audited, with the notice convening the meeting. The members can thus, even if they are unable to attend the meeting, study the accounts. A great deal of a club's money is spent on postage, and in these days of high postal charges this can be a considerable amount. Club secretaries—who work extremely hard for practically no reward—must answer any letter they receive from a member or would-be member; must send out notices of meetings; must forward to their chairman or to the treasurer anything which requires their attention. Treasurers must write receipts for all subscriptions. Sometimes members send too much or too little money, which means additional letters, though some members will help the club by sending postage. The officers of the club must write to each other, and sometimes to other committee members who have undertaken to do some special job. They have sometimes to send letters to their governing body, or to journals connected with feline matters. All this makes postage a big item on the balance sheet, although bi-annual reminders are no longer sent to members who have not paid.

A fair amount of a club's money must be spent on stationery and on duplicating; notepaper and envelopes, notices of meetings, agenda papers, balance sheets, rule books—all these cost money. However careful of the funds the secretary and treasurer may be, there are bound to be telephone calls, some of them long-distance, and extras, such as flowers for a member who is in hospital, registration of trophies to be sent by post and so on; the club's cups and trophies will have to be insured, and there will be an annual affiliation fee to be paid to the governing body. The big clubs such as the Siamese Cat Club have the same expenses on a much bigger scale besides running championship shows.

Money, however, is not the only consideration; there is a lot of work involved in running a club and the secretary—nearly always an honorary secretary—does by far the greater part of it. One of the advantages to owners of the cats of belonging to a club is that they can obtain information from the committee; the addresses of secretaries of governing bodies, lists of forthcoming shows, cats at stud, good boarding kennels or quarantine kennels—all these are matters about which a club secretary will put members in the way of obtaining information. Even genetic questions are asked of the secretary; he does not always know anything of this science himself, but he is almost sure to be able to put an enquirer in touch with some fellow club member who can answer the question asked. Besides dealing with such correspondence as this, the secretary has the work of calling meetings, seeing to the hire of suitable rooms, ordering tea for the annual general meeting, making sure that proper notices are sent out, and agenda papers correctly prepared. The treasurer will deal with all matters relating to club monies, but except where a committee member is appointed to do the work, it is the secretary who deals with the question of trophies and cups.

This is not at all an easy job. The actual trophies will be the responsibility of the treasurer, who will probably place them with the bank which has the club's account; but the secretary will keep a cup book, will receive requests from show managers for support, and will offer the club's trophies at the various shows. Club secretaries may arrange for advertisements of their clubs' activities to appear in show catalogues, though it is sometimes thought by the smaller clubs that to guarantee a class will bring the club to peoples' notice, and will be advertisement enough. The secretary will undertake on the club's behalf to guarantee classes at shows. Sometimes he will call a committee meeting to discuss these matters; it is important to a small club that not too much of its money be paid out on guaranteed classes; however, not only is it important for the club to be well represented in the show catalogues, but these 'club classes' are especially for the members, who naturally expect and appreciate them. The secretary may ask for a decision from his committee but, as a rule, it is he who knows what support should be offered at which shows. Nor is this work finished when the offers of support have been sent to the show manager; it is agreeable for members to be able to enter their cats and kittens in classes guaranteed by their own club; they may win small money prizes or rosettes or special prizes of one sort or another; but the club secretary, who will receive a marked catalogue from the show manager after the show, must watch carefully to be sure that winners are indeed members of the club. There are plenty of such pitfalls for the unwary, besides the rather lengthy work of adding points gained by owners of winning cats towards acquiring, for a season or maybe even outright, a given cup or trophy.

The work of a club chairman does not look onerous; but anyone who has had to do with a bad chairman will know how important it is to appoint a good one. A chairman should know thoroughly the rules of his club and of the governing body to which it is affiliated; he should have a good memory for past meetings and for the minutes of these. He should be able to give a ruling whenever necessary; he must be impartial: while being able to prevent any irregularity of procedure, he must never be biased. He must be strong—able firmly to stop any dissension which may arise at a meeting; if he conforms with all those things, he will be respected—if he happens to be a charming person he will be liked as well.

29 Champion red-point "Darling Dream Angus", owned by Mrs T Rimmer of Sutton Valence, Kent, England

30 Chocolate-point kitten "Essayci Tamora", owned by Miss Anderson-Kaine of Slough, Buckinghamshire, England

31 Seal-point "Djaména de Narisara", bred by Mme. Deucher of Bern and owned by Mme. Walther de Bons of Domdidier, Switzerland

32 Cream-point kitten "Mister Darcy". Owner: Dr Ritchie of Crookham, Hampshire, England

33 Red-point of wonderful type

34 Champion chocolate tortie-point "Cheongsun Jamida", owned by Mrs Daphne Deakin of Reading, Berkshire, England

35 Tortie-point "Ailsa Giempsa". Owners: Mr and Mrs Barnes of Bournemouth, Hampshire, England

36 Seal-point "Taishun Masterpiece", owned by Mrs N L Copland of Ashburton, New Zealand and bred by Mrs Edith Menezes in England

37 Grand Champion seal-point "Tellassee Ramona" owned and bred by Mrs N L Copland of Ashburton, New Zealand

38 Si-Rex "Sirafen Sangre Bleu", owned and bred by Mr and Mrs L H Wakeford of Wombourne, Staffordshire, England

39 "Annelida Evita", a cream-point Cornish Si-Rex, owned and bred by Alison Ashford of Maidstone, Kent, England

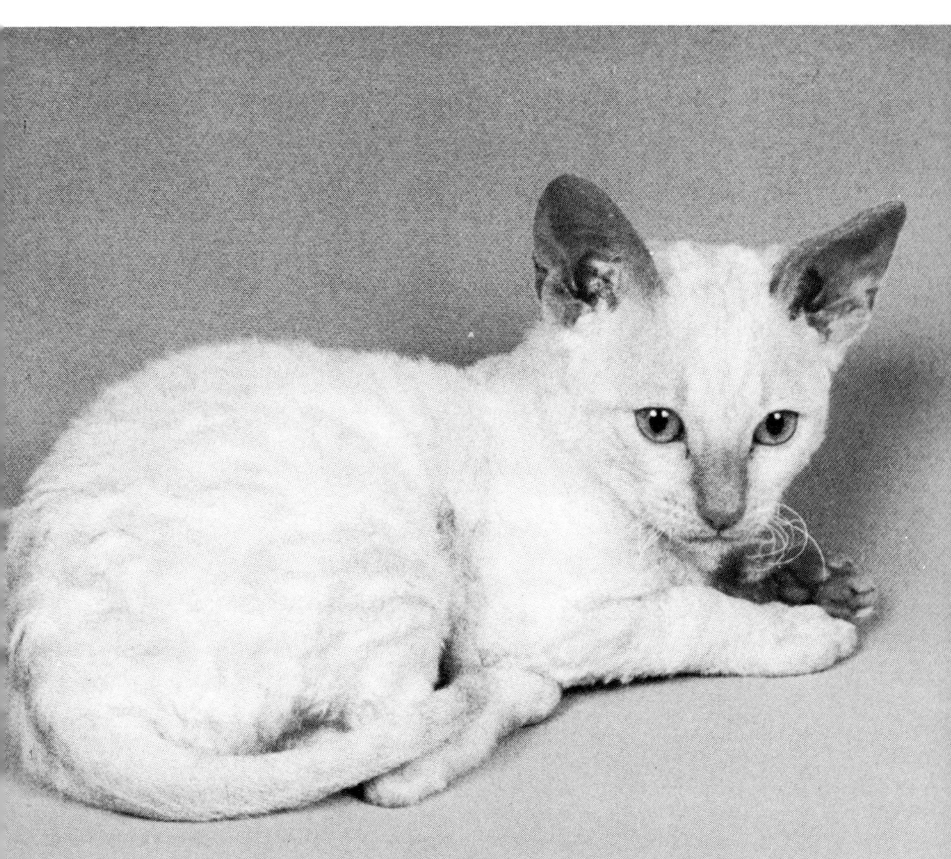

40 Head of "Darling Dream Angus" (see plate no. 29)

But the right sort of chairman must do his duty by his club and its membership regardless of his own popularity.

The work done by the officers and committee of a cat club brings to the members the shows, the prizes to be won, the information they require, the meetings that can interest them; very often the luncheon-party or tea-party where they can enjoy what has been described as 'catty-chatter'. As with all hobbies, a club brings its members together; and in addition to the pleasures of winning trophies or talking endlessly and very happily about Siamese cats and kittens, the members find that the serious matters of the fancy are dealt with by and through the clubs. An example is the question of help for the less fortunate felines; not only the big clubs but quite small ones, if they have a favourable bank balance at the end of the year, will invite members at a general meeting to vote a sum to be donated to veterinary research, or to some such organization as, in Britain, the Cat's Protection League. Lest anyone should think that these gifts do not benefit Siamese cats, it is worth noting that a surprising number of Siamese go through the hands of the Cats' Protection League: not only does this organization help greatly in restoring lost Siamese to frantic owners, it also finds suitable homes for many who have plainly been abandoned. This is a sad commentary on human nature—but it is true; the charming little 'status symbol' grows up, proves to be a female, produces half-bred kittens—and is turned out to fend for herself and for her unwanted progeny. The money given by the clubs to charitable institutions concerned with cats does indeed benefit Siamese; and money given to veterinary research, naturally, helps Siamese as much as it does other cats.

### THE GOVERNING COUNCIL IN BRITAIN

One of the most important functions of a club is that it is the link between its members and the governing body to which it is affiliated. In Britain, there is only one governing body—the Governing Council of the Cat Fancy; it is a good example of procedure, for in respect of affiliation there are no great variations as between one country and another. The Governing Council consists of delegates from the clubs. Any cat club with a membership of 100 may apply for affiliation and, when this and representation are granted, appoint a delegate who will attend Council meetings—four in a year. Once a club has attained a membership of 150, application may be made for a second delegate; and in any case, a substitute delegate may be appointed who can be called upon to attend if for any reason the club's official delegate is unable to be present at a Council meeting. Such procedure, or similar procedure is usual for governing bodies in all countries, and its importance lies in the fact that the Council consists of delegates from the clubs, and thus may be said truly to represent the views of the clubs. So far as the Siamese clubs in Britain are concerned, the Siamese Cat Club has two delegates, the Siamese Cat Association has two, and all the other clubs which cater for Siamese are represented. It will be seen that the interests of Siamese cats and their owners are well looked-after in the Governing Council.

### GOVERNING BODIES IN EUROPE

Siamese are more numerous in France than in any other European country, and France has a great many cat clubs. There are quite a few governing bodies: the Cercle Félin de Paris, the Association Féline de France, the Association Féline du Centre; the biggest is the Federation Internationale Féline d'Europe, known as FIFE. This federation has in fact clubs and associations affiliated to it in many countries from Italy up to Finland. There are now affiliated to FIFE the Australian Cat Federation, and a club in Sao Paulo, so that this is now a world-wide organization. All these bodies cater for every breed of cat, including of course Siamese, which are always present in considerable numbers at the international all-breed shows which take place in the different countries. There are also specialist clubs: for instance, in Switzerland, the Société Suisse du chat Persan et Siamois; this society is not limited, as are some clubs on the continent, to any one town or district, but only to these two breeds—Persians and Siamese. Anyone in Switzerland may belong, provided he owns a longhair or a Siamese, but owners of cats which are just household pets are not eligible for membership.[1]

In Italy there is only one big association, known simply as The Cat Club; however, there are senior Italian international judges who are as knowledgeable about Siamese as are their counterparts from anywhere else. Very good shows take place in Holland and Belgium, where many people are 'cat-minded', plenty of them being 'Siamese-cat-minded'; the Antwerp Cat Club is the oldest in Europe, and has recently celebrated its 50th anniversary and held its 40th show—a beautifully-organized show with lovely exhibits brought from far and wide.

### GOVERNING BODIES IN AMERICA

There are now nine governing bodies for cats in the United States. As with many of the differences between America and Britain, this is probably partly caused by the geographical factor: when the Governing Council of the Cat Fancy meets in London, delegates can quite easily attend from the north and from Scotland; but the United States extend from the Atlantic to the Pacific, and from the Canadian border to Mexico. Despite the swiftness of air travel, it takes much longer for someone living in the deep south to go to a meeting in New York than it does for a Cornishman to attend one in London. The nine organizations with authority to impose their rules are the American Cat Association, the National Cat Fanciers Association, the American Cat Fanciers Association, the Cat Fanciers Federation, the Crown Cat Fanciers Federation, the Independent Cat Federation, the United Cat Fanciers, the Cat Fanciers Association, and the American Cat Council.

All these bodies register cats and sanction shows, appoint their own judges, and have their own rules and standards of points. The American Cat Association was the first cat organization to be founded in the USA, and the Cat Fanciers Association is the largest of these bodies. Clubs and minor associations are affiliated to one or more of these, and it is advisable for breeders to register their cats and their cattery-names (which approximate to the prefixes granted by the Governing Council in Britain) with as many as possible of the nine. The ninth Governing Body is the American Cat Council, an organization which holds many shows. There are, of course, arguments in favour of having only one Governing Body, as the Council in Britain; but Mrs Susie Page of the Pageant Cattery, well-known judge, writer and breeder, tells me that in the USA, the Cat Fancy is better served by having several. This is partly for the obvious reason of big distances, but there are other considerations: the Cat Fanciers Association, for instance, which is by far the largest and most influential organization, allows monorchids to be shown and to win championships—a curious state of affairs, since such a defect can be passed on to the progeny. Another reason why breeders prefer a choice of registering bodies is that this, creating competition, precludes the concentration of power in just a few hands.

Incidentally, in 1975 CFA started a system of no-vetting-in at their shows, and many smaller associations have followed suit; Mrs Page has exhibited many times at shows where there was no examination of exhibits by vet.-surgeons, and she has neither experienced trouble in her own cattery nor seen any sign of sick cats being shown.[2]

It is estimated that there are as many as 400 clubs in America; many of them are quite small and do not hold shows but they are represented on their particular governing bodies. Only a very few, perhaps no more than half-a-dozen, of these clubs are concerned with Siamese only.

Besides the nine governing bodies and the many clubs and societies affiliated to them, there is the Siamese Cat Society of America, which is probably unique. This society, having been inaugurated in 1909, has recently completed its sixtieth year; it was the first Siamese breed society in the United States and it is in every sense an independent society. As now constituted, it is in no way a governing body; it appoints no judges, promotes no shows, has no clubs affiliated to it; it exists simply for one purpose: 'To unite people with the single purpose to love and better the Siamese cat and improve the standard.' It has today a membership of 900. It offers prizes at shows, many of them abroad, and its members often correspond from faraway places, using whatever language each can best understand. Such an organization is a unifying factor, making for friendship and doing a great deal to achieve its object of bettering the lot of the cats.

## AUSTRALIA

The British standard of points is used in most Australian States, though not in New South Wales, whose one governing body, the RASCC, has entirely its own rules. Some of these rules are unusual and interesting; one feature is that there are no classes at any show for household pets. In addition to the six States, there is the small

Northern Territory, which has recently started a small fancy of its own. Victoria and Queensland each have three or four governing bodies, and in Victoria it is necessary to adhere to only one of these. The other States have each only one governing body. With anything so big as the Australian fancy is becoming, it is not surprising that there should be many clubs; this is not only a country but a continent, and as Britain has one governing body, so New South Wales and Queensland, for example, each have theirs.

In 1977 I toured Australia and New Zealand, where there are some very good Siamese, and big classes for them at important shows: at the Cat Club of Western Australia at Perth in July 1977 there was a large Siamese entry, and the Reserve Best Siamese, a red-pointed of high quality, had the delightful name Chialee Red Satin. This show took place in the Royal Show Hall, a splendid complex permanently in perfect order for exhibitions of animals of different kinds. In Adelaide, at the Feline Association of South Australia's Show, also in July, there were again plenty of Siamese, with exceptional blue-pointeds; this show was run in aid of crippled children, and a big donation was able to be made. In the same month there were shows in Sydney and in Melbourne; at Sydney the Siamese Cat Society of New South Wales held a very big show; here, however, the red-pointeds are not classified as Siamese but are judged separately as 'colourpoints'; there is, nevertheless, the Lynx, Tortie and Red-Point Club, whose members are breeding beautiful cats. The Nepean Society in Melbourne also had very good Siamese at its show, as did the Siamese and Shorthair Society of Queensland. Indeed the Siamese cats who live under the Southern Cross measure up very well with their counterparts in Europe, and are in beautiful condition: it is something to be able to say that I judged at six shows and only once saw an exhibit that was not perfectly groomed.

## NEW ZEALAND

The New Zealand Siamese Cat Association caters exclusively for Siamese. It is the only Siamese cat club in New Zealand; here there are no societies for one or other colour as, for instance, the clubs for blue-pointeds in England and in Australia. The Association is affiliated to the NZ Governing Council of the Cat Fancy, and it produces its own pedigree forms and its own magazine. There is a big and growing membership, and at the shows all the points colours are well represented. New Zealand has a main and a supplementary register; the red-pointeds, first bred by Mrs Kerr of Dunedin, have been on the main register for some years, as have the tabby-pointeds, which are bred to perfection; in 1977 at the Franklin show in Auckland the Best Opposite Sex exhibit was a beautiful chocolate-tabby-point male, Arabesque Tabaroo, and a prize offered for 'judge's Fancy' went to a charming blue-tabby-pointed. Mrs Sonja Wilkinson, who is an all-breed judge and New Zealand's foremost experimental breeder, tells me that the English Standard of Points is used; the red-pointeds, tortie-pointeds and tabby-pointeds are here—and it seems an excellent arrangement—given the breed-numbers 24, 24a, 24b and 24c as in Britain where, however, the tabby-pointeds, red-pointeds and tortie-pointeds are 32, 32a and 32b. Mrs Wilkinson describes classes not found elsewhere called Typeclasses; in these, all Siamese varieties compete against each other, and are judged only on type and conformation with colour not taken into account.

The Association has more than 50 perpetual trophies, and the rosettes awarded at its annual show are especially made in the USA and are flown in for the occasion. This is indeed an event worth attending, for here may be seen the very best of the NZ Siamese cat world. Those who admire these cats may well be grateful to the breeders of 30 years ago who rescued the New Zealand Siamese and made them into the lovely breed they are today.

### CANADA AND SOUTH AFRICA

The clubs and associations of Canada and South Africa have already been discussed in the previous chapter, in connection with showing in these two countries.

### SUB-COMMITTEES

The position for club members everywhere is that any of them can, through his committee, put forward his ideas, criticisms and suggestions. Sometimes such points, raised by individuals, are so unrealistic that the club committee will not entertain them, but very often they are of value, and will be put before the Council in the form of a proposal.

The work of the Councils embraces everything of any importance to cats. In Britain, for example, sub-committees are appointed to deal with finance, with genetics, with disciplinary matters; the welfare of cats in general is of great moment, and the question of show dates in relation to possible spread of infection is annually discussed. These matters are not peculiar to the Council: governing bodies all over the world are concerned with them. There is on the Governing Council a preponderance of delegates from the Siamese clubs, and this is simply because Siamese are the most popular breed of cat, and therefore are the concern of many clubs with many members. The delegates to the Council may be instructed by their clubs to support a given proposal, or to vote in a certain sense; this is one of the points that make the work of a delegate difficult: he is present at Council meetings to represent his club; if the club has voted in a given sense on any matter to be discussed in Council, then its delegate must regard this as an instruction to support the club's views at the Council meeting concerned. Of course, he could resign as delegate if he found himself unable to agree with his club's decision. Anyone wishing to join in his club's activities, and to be appointed to its committee, and to other committees, such as the Council or, in the case of Siamese in Britain the advisory committee which appoints Siamese judges, must be prepared to work.

There is a great deal to be done, and those ready to do it are the good committee members. Anyone who believes it will be grand to sit in the seats of the mighty but who is not prepared to do any work will be of no use. A delegate, for instance, to the Council, should be in a position to spare enough time to give careful thought to any matter on the agenda paper which may concern his club; to be ready to report to his club committee anything which directly concerns it, while never discussing Council matters with anyone at all unless they do concern his own committee. He may have to listen for a long time to discussions which are the affair of other clubs and which may hold no interest for him: it remains his duty to pay attention to whatever is under consideration, and to cast his vote with regard to what is fair and good for the cats, without thought of personalities. A club appoints whomsoever it approves as its delegate to the governing body or to any committee with which it is concerned, and it can, according to its rules, change its delegate if it so wishes; some clubs appoint their delegates through their committees, others at their Annual General Meeting. It can therefore truly be said that the decisions of the governing body are those of the clubs themselves.

### CLUB JOURNALS

Of great value are the journals produced by the clubs. Perhaps the most successful is the *Siamese News Quarterly* of the Siamese Cat Society of America; the Society's aim is 'to unite people with the single purpose to love and better the Siamese cat', and its quarterly circles the globe, for it has a big membership which embraces every country, so that its journal goes all over the world. The Siamese Cat Club's *News Sheet* is nowadays duplicated, as are pretty-well all club journals, for the costs of printing are extremely high; it was at first printed on thick art paper and had beautiful illustrations; this was before the 1939 war and such people, now no longer young, as have kept copies, naturally treasure them; but the present *News Sheet* is at least as informative, and well-worth having—and keeping, as a record for the future. Club journals are legion, from the Siamese Cat Association's *Journal* to *Purr* of the Feline Association of Southern Australia, *Catcall*, Western Australia, *Lynx, Tortie and Redpoint*, Siamese Cat Society, New South Wales, or *On Target*, Siamese and Shorthair Society of Queensland.

There is in Britain a club which caters for new varieties—the Colourpoint, Rex and Any Other Variety Cat Club. Many a newly-evolved or newly-discovered breed has made its debut under the aegis of this club, often leaving its protection when it is fairly launched and has a club of its own: though it is primarily the Colourpoint Club, its committee is always willing to consider sponsoring whatever is new, and this club also runs a very successful journal. Such publications are not just a description of club meetings and a few sentimental articles, interesting to the members only; they are a record; they embrace the views of contemporary writers, some of them geneticists or biologists interested in veterinary research; and —a matter of great moment—they go to every country. America's *Siamese News Quarterly* is sent to its own members and copies of most club journals go to people not necessarily members, sent to them by friends, and making links in a world-wide chain of siamophiles. Articles in these periodicals are sometimes controversial, since people write to put forward contrary views; but they are never really unfriendly, not only because no editor would print an unpleasant letter, but by reason of the fact that most fanciers can appreciate the importance of discussion. It is in fact true that people who may quarrel about position or procedure will be at one in anything which concerns the cats. Basically, the only undesirable Siamese cat fancier is the one who neglects his cats; for those who are fond of their cats, the little club papers provide introductions of real value between people and countries.

## INTER-CLUB ACTIVITIES

Inter-club activities are many. Judges are often invited to take classes in countries not their own; Canada and America will exchange judges, and both America and countries in Europe as well as Australia often ask British judges to come and officiate at their shows; judges from other countries come to judge at British shows, and clubs will send trophies to be offered at shows run in other countries. Such international relations are, of course, not confined to Siamese, but the preponderance in numbers of these cats makes them conspicuous at any show where there are classes for them.

Novices naturally deliberate whether to join a club, or more than one club. Newcomers to the fancy in Britain will very often start off by becoming members of one of the big clubs: the Siamese Cat Club, or the Siamese Cat Association; they may then discover that there is a small club catering for their own particular favourite variety—maybe the Red-pointed Cat Club, or the Lilac-pointed Cat Club—and join that also. As you make friends in the fancy, so you will be invited to join other associations; probably it is a mistake to belong to too many: it is possible to find that you are entangled in 'cat politics', or have divided loyalties; perhaps to discover at the start of a new year that you resent having so many subscriptions to pay, and cannot spare the time to attend each and every annual general meeting. Very likely it is after all best to be a member of one of the big clubs and of the speciality club dealing with your particular choice in points-colour. The big clubs, of course, cater for every variety of Siamese; the Siamese Cat Club, the Siamese Cat Association, the Siamese Cat Society—there is no Siamese cat of any variety which does not come under their aegis.

### REGISTRATION IN AMERICA

In America, it is possible to get into difficulties due to the number of governing bodies; all can grant cattery names, and approve individual names for the cats; thus it is possible to register a kitten with one governing body under a cattery name granted by that body, and to find that there is another kitten appearing in the show ring and, later, perhaps advertised as a stud or a brood queen with precisely the same name and cattery name (prefix) granted by one of the other seven governing bodies. This is plainly not good for the owner of the better of the two kittens, who will find himself accused of breeding and maybe selling an inferior animal. Even if two such kittens should be of equal merit, the duplication of the name and cattery name is likely to cause confusion, and to avoid such occurrences, breeders of note feel themselves obliged to join more than one governing body, paying fees to perhaps as many as four, and registering their kittens with all of these, so as to be sure that no one else will be granted the same prefix and names. This, of course, is somewhat expensive and troublesome, and incidentally, duplication of names and cattery names could bedevil the future history of the breed where pedigrees are concerned. Probably in a country so large as the USA or Australia, distances to be travelled are in themselves a reason for the existence of more than one governing body, as mentioned above.

Registration in America must, nowadays, be carried out very carefully. The Cat Fanciers Association has forms requiring very full details, including narrow descriptions of eye-colour. These forms are accompanied by a list of extremely strict rules for registration, and also by very long lists of breeds which may be accepted for registration; in the section of this list devoted to Siamese appear red-points and gold-points (probably the dilute of red, known in Britain as cream-points).

CFA requires that litters shall be registered: litter registration is, since 1967, the only way in which a cat may be registered. It is necessary to register first the whole litter, and then the individual kittens, which would not be accepted for registration if the litter as a whole had not first been registered. If a Siamese queen's litter be sired by an unknown cat, or by a registered male of another breed, the new arrivals' names must go into a special register kept especially for recording the names of kittens not having three generations of like-to-like breeding behind them. A cross with an unknown or unregistered cat can bring in new strength, and is not a bad thing if the breeder can afford to rear some non-saleable kittens, and find good homes for them. However, if such a breeder intends to put one or more of these kittens back to Siamese, and endeavours to get back the Siamese type—as can be done with less difficulty than might be thought—they will have to be registered. Each governing body in the USA has a record which approximates to Britain's Supplementary Register and these are differently named: particularly appropriately designated is ACA's Ancestry Register; other names used for these registers are 'Foundation', 'Primary', 'Experimental', and 'Provisional'. ACA requires that a cat be in the Stud Book (approximating to Britain's Full Register) before becoming a champion. The reason for this is that it ought to be clearly seen that a champion has at least four generations of like breeding and will, mated to his like, produce only his like.

That recognition should not be awarded until the governing body concerned is very sure that the new variety is soundly established is necessary; the importance of registration lies in the fact that, for example, the Siamese correctly registered today, even if there be a bend sinister in his family tree, is part of the breed's future history.

## REGISTRATION IN BRITAIN

In Britain you can register any cat whose pedigree you do not know provided you are prepared to state that his or her ancestors are unregistered or unknown; such a cat's name will go in the Governing Council's Supplementary Register. The British have what is referred to as 'the three generations rule'; this requires that any kitten, to have his name in the Full Register, must have three generations of like breeding behind him. Thus the lilac-points, when they first appeared, were registered in the Supplementary Register; they were bound to breed true, since the character is recessive: lilac-point to lilac-point could produce only lilac-pointed kittens; but only when a kitten's pedigree could be presented to the Council showing his two parents, four grandparents and eight great-grandparents all lilac-pointed could his name go in the Full Register. This has nothing to do with 'recognition'; a breed is recognised and given a number at the Council's will and pleasure—which is to say when the breed or variety is firmly established. But any cat may be registered: you can take in a little black stray, cross him with a champion Siamese female, and register his kittens in the Supplementary Register.

It has been suggested that the system of registration should be still further broken down, so that there shall be not only a main register and a supplementary register, but three classes of registration: one for cats whose parents, grandparents and great-grandparents, though all of the same breed are not necessarily all of the same variety; one for cats whose immediate ancestors show two cats of different breeds; and one for cats one or more of whose immediate forebears are unregistered or unknown.

It is doubtful whether the Governing Council will ever accept this suggestion. It is in any case plain that the adoption of this proposal would make practically no difference in the registration of Siamese.

Owners of longhair Smokes, and Chinchillas, necessarily bred from Silver Tabbies, could find this a big alteration; and for the Tortoiseshells, quite unable to have male ancestors of their own breed, or for Manx who must have some tailed forbears, this might be an awkward changeover. For the Siamese, however, all of the same breed no matter what the colour of their points, such an innovation would make little or no difference.

Sometimes, in Britain, fanciers speak of the one governing body as having 'a monoply', but the contrary view, the view that it is fortunate to have only one such body is almost certainly the right one. With one Council, no confusion arises, and delegates from all the clubs confer in Council together. Owners of cats pay no annual subscription to the Governing Council; they pay a fee if they wish to have a prefix; this will be granted in perpetuity. When at a Council meeting, new requests for prefixes are read out by the secretary, a very great deal of trouble is taken by the delegates to make sure not merely that the same prefix shall not twice be granted—this should have appeared from the records before the matter need come before the Council—but that the prefix to be granted shall not too closely resemble an existing one, let alone be identical. No individual pays any sort of subscription to the Governing Council. You pay a fee that buys your prefix in perpetuity and you pay a fee, through the registrar, whenever you register any kittens—this fee is smaller for those who have their own prefix; you pay—again through the registrar—if you require verification of a pedigree or information on a pedigree; there is also a fee payable for a Governing Council certified pedigree for a kitten to be sold abroad: this certificate will be required by the governing body in the country to which the kitten is to be exported and it is, normally, the purchaser's business to pay for it.

The annual number of requests for registration of Siamese is so great that one registrar deals with this breed only, while two other registrars deal with longhairs and all other shorthairs.

Fees to the Council are paid by the clubs: a fee of £2.50p. for each delegate plus a per capita fee for members. The full Council meets four times a year, but there is an executive committee appointed annually by the delegates from their numbers, as well as the several other committees dealing with genetics, discipline—which concerns infraction of rules—finance, and so on. It can happen that people may become impatient, or disapproving of some Council decision; but the Council is the voice of the clubs and its decisions are the vote of the clubs. Any society not satisfied has the remedy: to send the strongest, most experienced delegate available.

## NATIONAL CLUBS AND ASSOCIATIONS

It is not easy to give a simple list of societies catering exclusively for Siamese cats, since the position in this respect varies greatly from one country to another.

In Great Britain the matter is easy enough; there exist:

*The Siamese Cat Club*, the largest specialist cat club in the world.
*The Siamese Cat Society of the British Empire.*
*The Blue-pointed Siamese Cat Club.*
*The Chocolate-pointed Siamese Cat Club.*
*The Siamese Cat Association.*
*The Lilac-pointed Siamese Cat Club.*
*The Red-pointed Siamese Cat Club.*
*The Tabby-pointed Siamese Cat Club.*
*The Northern Siamese Cat Club.*
*The Tabby-pointed Society.*
*The Seal-pointed Siamese Cat Club.*

Some of these are very old-established, others have not been very long in being; but all, even the small clubs which hold no shows and have memberships of 200 or even less, are well-established.

On the continent of **Europe**, there is no lack of cat clubs, a great many affiliated to the *Federation Internationale Féline d'Europe* (FIFE), and a good many which are independent of any affiliation; but these are, for the most part, all-breed clubs. There is in Switzerland the *Société du Chat Persan et Siamois*: even in this case the longhairs and the Siamese are sharing a society.

In the **USA** the position is complicated; small clubs catering for Siamese only arise and fall—attached during their brief day and with their membership of maybe only 20-30 to one or other of the big governing bodies. Here, however, there is the Siamese Cat Society of America. This very important society runs no shows, is entirely independent, has a membership not far short of 1,000, and exists for Siamese only.

In **Australia** there are several clubs catering for Siamese:

*The Siamese Cat Society of New South Wales.*

*The Lynx, Tortie and Red-Point Club.*

*The Siamese and Shorthair Society of Queensland.*

**New Zealand** has but one club dedicated to Siamese, the important:

*New Zealand Siamese Cat Association.*

All the above have, naturally, secretaries. The best way to reach them is to buy a copy of *Fur and Feather* (the official organ of the Governing Council of the Cat Fancy) and write to a likely-seeming address, enclosing a stamped, addressed envelope and asking for information. A list of names and addresses, correct as I write, might be incorrect and therefore misleading by the time this text reaches the printer. For though it sometimes seems that brilliant club secretaries are like fixed stars, there are many reasons why they may, overnight, give place to others.

The many associations formed for cats throughout the world may be specialist organizations, such as Britain's Red, Cream and Tortoiseshell Cat Club; but those—and they are many—which do not specialize always cater for Siamese: as for instance the Cat Club of Antwerp. This, anywhere at all in the world, is the strength of the clubs: that the fancy is, in the last analysis, governed by the clubs themselves and their members. And by far the most important work carried out by clubs and councils alike is the work of aiding and protecting the cats. It may be thought that the cat in need of care is only the poor moggie left to stray; but this is not so: not only are Siamese sometimes abandoned, but they are peculiarly vulnerable in another way; people who love money more than they do cats are able to exploit Siamese simply because these cats are popular; such unscrupulous people buy two or three queens, not necessarily of good quality, and a male to match; as fast as kittens arrive they are advertised for low prices and sold off as young as possible for what they will fetch to purchasers who want a 'prestige' cat. This involves mass-production, with a 'small profits, quick returns' method of sale, there is nothing illegal in it unless it involves cruelty—but it very often does. Crowded conditions, lack of cleanliness, queens who are treated just as machines; sometimes matters get out-of-hand and then the conditions under which the cats are kept really defy description. The Governing Council has no jurisdiction over anyone not a member of one of its affiliated clubs, but a great deal of good has been done by it in cases of this kind, and the Royal Society for Prevention of Cruelty to Animals is always very helpful. As is in the USA the American Society for Prevention of Cruelty to Animals. Here there are also the very large Humane Association, the SPCA Boston and the SPCA Massachussetts. In addition, Britain and Massachusetts together founded the International Society for Prevention of Cruelty to Animals, Known as ISPA, with which were joined, besides the USA, Denmark and Germany, and which has now coordinated 82 societies in 35 countries. All of these bodies will tender help to any governing body in the cat world which asks for it.

The Siamese cat clubs are societies of people with the same interest who can, if they organize their affairs well, wield considerable power for good and for the betterment of the conditions of the cats.

With their arrival in Queensland, the Siamese cats are facing Malaysia whence they came. And those who care for them and handle them will probably agree that they have brought nothing but good.

# References

CHAPTER 1

1. A. G. Searle *Comparative Genetics of Coat-Colour in Mammals*
2. Ibid.
3. Letter to the Author dated 8 September 1969 from the British Embassy, Bangkok
4. Note in the author's possession written by Sir Owen O'Malley.
5. From a letter to the Author from the British Embassy, Bangkok.
6. Letter to the Author from Khunying Abhibal Rajmaitri written in 1969.
7. *Cats Magazine* 1969, Siamese section of a history of the American cat fancy, compiled by Charles A. Kenny reprinted in the *Siamese News Quarterly Inc.*
8. Ibid.
9. From a letter written to the Author by Mrs Sonja Wilkinson, President of the New Zealand Siamese Cat Association Inc.
10. From an article by Margaret B. Dale in the Siamese Cat Clubs *News Sheet* September, 1950.
11. Ibid.
12. Letter to the Author from M. N. Batten.

CHAPTER 2

1. A. G. Searle *Comparative Genetics of Coat-Colour in Mammals*
2. From an article written in 1950 by the late Miss Wentworth-Fitzwilliam.

CHAPTER 3

1. Sir Arthur Keith.
2. A. G. Searle.

CHAPTER 5

1. J. W. H. Holmes, MRCVS, DVS.
2. *Animal Health A Centenary 1865–1965*, Her Majesty's Stationary Office 1965.
3. Extract from veterinary record dated 9 August 1969.
4. Information from Mr Turner of Shurlock Row Quarantine Cattery.

CHAPTER 6

1. From a letter written to the Author by Mrs Linda Emery, South Africa's Registrar and foremost breeder and judge.
2. Extract from a letter written by Mrs Eve Gower of Rotorua, New Zealand.

CHAPTER 8

1. From a letter written to the Author by Mrs Linda Emery.

CHAPTER 9

1. From a letter to the Author from Madame Pia Hollenstein, President of the Société Suisse du chat Persan et Siamois, and International judge.
2. Letter to the Author from Mrs Susie Page of the USA.

# Glossary

*Affiliation.* Attachment—i.e. of a small club to a big federation.
*Agouti.* The original wild-type mammalian coat-pattern with banded hairs of black, brown and yellow.
*Ailurophile.* Friendly towards cats. Noun, one who loves cats.
*Albino.* An organism completely unable to produce pigment.
*Allele.* One gene of two or more at the same locus which have the same or differing phenotypic effects, being inherited from both parents.
*Amino-acid.* One of many specific types of organo-acids each able to reproduce varied effects.
*Antibodies.* Protective cells present in an organism to control deleterious germs.
*Ascaris.* Roundworm.
*Astronomical.* To do with the stars.
*Backcross.* The mating of a heterozygote to a homozygote.
*Chromosomes.* Cells existing in pairs and which make up living tissue.
*Cline.* Continuing gradient over a geographical area of a particular form of life.
*Dilution.* A variation in colour to produce a weaker shade. i.e. cream is the dilute of red.
*Diploid.* With two sets of chromosomes, the normal situation before cell-division.
*Dominant.* Showing in the phenotype in the heterozygote.
*Endemic.* Belonging to a particular country.
*Epistatic.* Masking the phenotypic effects of another, non-allelic gene; i.e. white, in the coat-colour of a cat, is sometimes a mask for another colour.
*Eumelanin.* Brown or black pigment.
*Gamete.* The sex cell—the spermatozoon or the ovum.
*Gene.* Unit of life, carried on the chromosomes and governing the various characters of the organism concerned.
*Genotype.* The genetic make-up of an organism in respect of a given character.
*Gestation.* The period of time between fertilisation and birth.
*Heterozygous.* Having different alleles at a given locus, e.g. one for blue and one for brown.

*Homozygous*. Having the same alleles at a given locus.
*Hybrid*. In the present sense, a heterozygote; in the old sense, a cross between two species.
*Inbreeding*. The mating of close relatives.
*Inoculation*. Treatment by insertion into the body.
*Locus*. The position of a given gene on a particular chromosome.
*Mastitis*. Inflammation of the mammary glands.
*Melanocyte*. A cell containing pigment—the pigment cell.
*Mezozoic*. A period in geological time which ended approximately 55 million years ago, and which lasted approximately 135 million years.
*Mutation*. Change in the structure of heredity.
*Neural Crest*. A region of the brain whence cells proliferate in the embryo.
*Onyxectomy*. A surgical operation for removal of a nail or nails from an organism.
*Ovum*. The female cell for reproduction—the egg.
*Palaeontology*. The science of past geological periods.
*Panleucopenia*. A condition of the blood stream commonly known as feline infectious enteritis.
*Parasite*. An organism using another as host upon which to subsist.
*Pelage*. Fur.
*Phaeomelanin*. Yellow or red pigment.
*Phenotype*. The appearance of an organism in respect of a given character.
*Pigment-granules*. The colour-bearing granules, carried in the pigment cells.
*Progeny*. Offspring.
*Rage*. Fr. Rabies, hydrophobia.
*Recessive*. With no phenotypic effect in the heterozygote.
*Saurian*. Resembling a lizard; a prehistoric animal.
*Sex-linkage*. Attachment to one only of the sex chromosomes.
*Sperm*. Spermatozoon; the male gamete.
*Sterility*. Inability to reproduce.
*Striations*. Stripes.
*Subcutaneous*. Under the skin.
*Svelte*. Slender.
*Trilobite*. An early marine organism, minute, and having three lobes.
*Vaccine*. A preparation made from dead or a-virulent disease germs and used as a protection against the disease concerned.
*Virus*. Minute organism causing disease in the larger organism which it uses as host.
*Zygote*. Fertilised ovum with the diploid number of chromosomes restored.

# Index